C000083675

The ultimate fan guide to

RUPAUL'S DRAG RACE

The ultimate fan guide to

RUPAUL'S DRAG RACE

John Davis
Illustrated by Paul Borchers

Smith Street Books

CONTENTS

RuPaul

"Once upon a time there was a little black boy born and raised in San Diego, California, who at 15 moved to Atlanta to study Performance Art and then went on to become the most famous supermodel in the world."

RuPaul Andre Charles was a boy who always liked to play with all of the colours from the crayon box. Affirmed by his mother from an early age that he was going to be a star, RuPaul was given his unique first name by her because "ain't another motherfucker alive with a name like that". After moving out of home to pursue a career in the entertainment industry studying at the North Atlanta School of Performing Arts in his teens, Ru soon dropped out knowing he needed to find his calling – something that would utilise his effervescent personality and incomparable charm.

A Jack-of-all-trades from the outset, RuPaul of the early 1980s led a punk rock band called Wee Wee Pole, go-go danced on bars, presented a cable access political gay talk show and hosted numerous local events as a smeared-lipstick, combat-boot-wearing, anti-establishment type of performer. Once the Atlanta scene grew tired for RuPaul, he moved to New York, chasing his own star on the rise with other Atlanta nightlife notables Larry Tee and Lady Bunny. Teaming up with his hometown club family in New York, RuPaul began creating the original "Starrbooty" series, a pastiche of 1960s blaxploitation films, which were distributed in the nightclubs he performed in, before discovering that his dreams of super-stardom in the Big Apple were harder to reach than anticipated. After struggling for the best part of the 80s and his several moves from couch to couch and back across the country to live with his sister, Ru resettled in New York in 1989 determined to change up his act to become RuPaul the glamazon.

Following his crowning as the Queen of Manhattan in 1989 and a guest appearance in The B-52's music video for "Love Shack", RuPaul swiftly changed gears and began his ascendancy by signing with record label Tommy Boy and recording his debut studio album *Supermodel of the World*. The lead single "Supermodel (You

Better Work)" was released in November 1992 and became a hit in the US and across Europe making RuPaul, the 6'7" man in drag, a household name. In the years following, RuPaul hosted the MTV Video Music Awards and the Brit Awards (with Sir Elton John) and released a UK #7 hit single with Sir Elton – a cover of the 70s hit "Don't Go Breaking My Heart" produced by disco legend Giorgio Moroder. Modelling contracts with makeup giant M.A.C. Cosmetics and a book release (*Lettin It All Hang Out* in 1995) kept Ru's star on the rise throughout the mid 1990s before he began hosting his own talk show, *The RuPaul Show*, with radio hostess Michelle Visage in 1996. A melting pot of A-list celebrity interviews, live performances and even political discussions, *The RuPaul Show* ran for 100 episodes over two seasons and allowed Ru to meet and perform alongside many of his childhood idols including Cher and Diana Ross. Finishing off the decade with a guest starring role in *The Brady Bunch* remake film and a legendary duet of "It's Raining Men" with another of his idols, Martha Wash, RuPaul was about to embark on the third phase of his drag career – going underground again.

Faced with the post-9/11 Republican world at his doorstep, RuPaul made the creative and professional decision to take a break from showbiz after what was an incredibly successful run. Quietly releasing studio and remix albums as well as the odd club single between 2004 and 2008, RuPaul, the "Supermodel of the World", was faced with a lack of promotion and support from the industry that built him up only 10 years prior. Armed with a new outlook on his place in the universe, RuPaul began working on a new television opportunity, inspired by the success of Tyra Banks' *America's Next Top Model*.

RuPaul's Drag Race aired its first season in 2009 on LGBT-focused lifestyle cable channel Logo TV and the rest is herstory. Going from strength to strength over 10 main cycles and four *All Stars* seasons between 2009 and 2019, *Drag Race* harnessed the revisiting of 1990s pop culture in mainstream society. Bringing together fierce drag competitors from across the US, Puerto Rico and even Australia to a gauntlet where sewing, performance, styling and comedy skills are tested to discover America's Next Drag Superstar, RuPaul created a whole new world of drag aspiration. Incorporation of new RuPaul dance anthems like "Glamazon", "Sissy That Walk" and "Cover Girl" into the programming, allowed for new fans of his music to jump on board the train that started two decades earlier. As the popularity of the show and viewership increased from season to season, RuPaul created RuPaul's DragCon in 2015, the first ever convention focused on drag queens, their artistry and cultural impact. With new found mainstream appeal in the show and drag artistry on the whole, it only made sense that RuPaul would soon be snatching his own titles and has earned his own star on the Hollywood Walk of Fame and three (!) Primetime Emmy Awards for Outstanding Host for a Reality or Reality-Competition Program. RuPaul, the ultimate glamazon, supermodel and all round Queen Bee isn't showing signs of slowing down... And neither are his girls.

RuFacts & Figures

The MOGUL

RU-ENTERPRISE MERCHANDISE:
RuPaul Limited Edition Collector's Figurine

"Glamazon" fragrance by Colorevolution

RuPaul Bar (peanut butter and sea salt chocolate
bar) from SWEET! candy store, Hollywood

Lettin It All Hang Out (biography)

Workin' It! (self help guide)

WHICH RU ARE YOU?:
RuPaul as Mrs. Cummings
(*The Brady Bunch Movie*, 1995)

RuPaul as Rachel Tensions
(*To Wong Foo, Thanks for Everything!
Julie Newmar*, 1995)

RuPaul as Starrbooty
(*Starrbooty*, 2007)

RuPaul as Tyrell Tyrelle
(*Another Gay Sequel: Gays Gone Wild!*, 2008)

RuPaul as Rudolph
(*Ugly Betty*, 2010)

RuPaul as Marcel
(*Broad City*, 2017)

The ALBUMS

SELECTED DISCOG-RU-PHY:
*RuPaul is Star Booty:
Original Motion Picture Soundtrack* (1986)

Supermodel of the World (1993)

Foxy Lady (1996)

Ho, Ho, Ho (1997)

RuPaul's Go-Go Box Classics (1998)

Red Hot (2004)

*Starrbooty: Original Motion
Picture Soundtrack* (2007)

Champion (2009)

Glamazon (2011)

Born Naked (2014)

Realness (2015)

Greatest Hits (2015)

Slay Belles (2015)

Butch Queen (2016)

American (2017)

*Remember Me:
Essential*, Volumes 1 & 2 (2017)

Christmas Party (2018)

The SINGLES

SELECTED SINGLES:
"Supermodel (You Better Work)" (1992)

"A Shade Shady (Now Prance)" (1993)

"Don't Go Breaking My Heart"
(with Elton John) (1993)

"Looking Good, Feeling Gorgeous" (2004)

"Cover Girl" (2009)

"Peanut Butter" (featuring Big Freedia) (2012)

"Sissy That Walk" (2014)

"Read U, Wrote U" (with Alaska, Detox,
Katya & Roxxxy) (2016)

"Call Me Mother" (2018)

"American" (with Aquaria, Asia,
Eureka & Kameron) (2018)

The LOOKS

Soul Train Sister by RuPaul as seen
in the B-52's music video for
"Love Shack"

Confederate Flag Dress by Marlene Stewart,
as seen in *To Wong Foo, Thanks for Everything!
Julie Newmar*

Isis Winged Showgirl by Bob Mackie, as seen at
the 1995 VH1 Fashion and Music Awards

Golden Glamazon by Zaldy, as seen in *RuPaul's
Drag Race* Season 4 promo

Panther on the Runway by Zaldy, as seen in
RuPaul's Drag Race Season 6 promo

Supermodel of the World by Zaldy, as seen in the
music video for "Supermodel (You Better Work)"

SIGNATURE LOOK:
Supermodel of the World Realness

TYPE:
The Glamazon

Top Toots of the Season

SEASON 1:
Shannel's Medusa,
Episode 3 "Queens of All Media"

SEASON 2:
Tyra Sanchez's Wedding Couture,
Episode 5 "Here Comes the Bride"

SEASON 3:
Raja's Marie Antoinette,
Episode 4 "Totally Leotarded"

SEASON 4:
Sharon Needles' Post-Apocalyptic Couture,
Episode 1 "RuPocalypse Now!"

SEASON 5:
Roxxxy Andrews' Deadliest Snatch Glamor Swimsuit,
Episode 5 "Snatch Game"

SEASON 6:
Courtney Act's Animal Kingdom Bird Couture,
Episode 9 "Drag Queens of Talk"

SEASON 7:
Violet Chachki's Death Becomes Her Corset,
Episode 6 "Ru Hollywood Stories"

SEASON 8:
Naomi Smalls' Book Couture,
Episode 8 "RuPaul Book Ball"

SEASON 9:
Valentina's Mariachi Plaza Hometown Look,
Episode 1 "Oh. My. Gaga!"

SEASON 10:
Kameron Michaels' Feather Fantasy,
Episode 3 "Tap That App"

ALL STARS SEASON 1:
Raven's Super Villain Couture,
Episode 5 "Dynamic Drag Duos"

ALL STARS SEASON 2:
Detox's Latex Eleganza,
Episode 2 "All Stars Snatch Game"

ALL STARS SEASON 3:
Shangela's Christmas RuDemption Look,
Episode 2 "Divas Lip Sync Live"

ALL STARS SEASON 4:
Manila Luzon's Eleguence After Dark,
Episode 2 "Super Girl Groups, Henny"

Top Boots of the Season

SEASON 1:
Rebecca Glasscock's KISS Couture,
Episode 4 "M.A.C. Viva-Glam Challenge"

SEASON 2:
Mystique Summers Madison's Country Couture,
Episode 3 "Country Queens"

SEASON 3:
Shangela's Fantasy Hair Outfit,
Episode 11 "RuPaul's Hair Extravaganza"

SEASON 4:
Jiggly Caliente's Post-Apocalyptic Couture,
Episode 1 "RuPocalypse Now!"

SEASON 5:
Serena ChaCha's Dumpster Dive Lederhosen,
Episode 1 "RuPaullywood or Bust"

SEASON 6:
Kelly Mantle's Downton Abbey Bacon Dress,
Episode 1 "RuPaul's Big Opening"

SEASON 7:
Kennedy Davenport's Hello Kitty Eleganza,
Episode 11 "Hello, Kitty Girls!"

SEASON 8:
Derrick Barry's Tinman,
Episode 6 "Wizards of Drag"

SEASON 9:
Nina Bo'Nina Brown's Bunny Makeover,
Episode 10 "Makeovers: Crew Better Work"

SEASON 10:
Dusty Ray Bottoms' Feather Fantasy,
Episode 3 "Tap That App"

ALL STARS SEASON 1:
Mimi Imfurst's "Dead Muppets" Couture,
Episode 1 "It Takes Two"

ALL STARS SEASON 2:
Alyssa Edwards' 2-in-1 Camera Dress,
Episode 4 "Drag Movie Shequels"

ALL STARS SEASON 3:
Shangela's Studio 54 Disco Look,
Episode 5 "Pop Art Ball"

ALL STARS SEASON 4:
Trinity The Tuck's LaLaPaRUza Outfit,
Episode 6 "LaLaPaRUza"

The Gag of the Season

SEASON 1: "LIFE IS A CELEBRATION!"

Ongina's reveal of being HIV positive not only made for compelling reality television but was also able to bring to a prime-time queer audience the urgency needed to understand, respect and support those in our immediate community who are being discriminated upon based on their health status.

SEASON 2: "WHY ARE YOU TALKING?"

Tyra Sanchez and Tatianna's feud in the "Here Comes the Bride" episode not only revealed Tyra's bratty side to the judges and the audience, but delivered one of the most iconic throws under the bus ever seen on *Drag Race* and solidified Tatianna as not just a pretty face but a formidable queen of telling the tea.

SEASON 3: "DRAG IS NOT A CONTACT SPORT!"

Mimi Imfurst's bold and brash lifting of India Ferrah into the high heavens and carrying her from the judge's desk back to the stage during their iconic lip sync, drew the ire of RuPaul and allegedly changed the rules about being able to step off the main stage during a lip sync.

SEASON 4: "WHAT DID WILLAM DO?"

Drag Race's wild child Willam to this day remains the only contestant to be disqualified from the race for breaking rules that keep the competition fair – in the same episode he won the maxi challenge! Stupefying the bottom two lip syncers Phi Phi O'Hara and Sharon Needles who gave an electrifying and wig-flipping battle on the main stage, Willam left the competition, vomit-filled umbrella and all, leaving audiences asking: "What did Willam Do?".

SEASON 5: "WE AS GAY PEOPLE GET TO CHOOSE OUR FAMILY"

Truly iconic and game changing lip syncs don't happen everyday... unless you're Roxxxy Andrews and Alyssa Edwards. In a lip sync battle that sees shoes falling apart and wild dance routines, it's Roxxxy's now iconic wig reveal that floored the Season 5 queens, RuPaul and audiences alike. The epic lip sync was followed by an unexpected breakdown from Roxxxy, revealing that she was abandoned by her mother as a child at a bus stop. Fierce strong queens deserve second chances and not a single queen went home that week.

SEASON 6: "I FEEL VERY ATTACKED!"

Death-dropping into the season with her head and disposition higher "than your receding hairline", Laganja Estranja made it clear that she was ready to get sickening. As the difficulty of the challenges wore on her confidence, Laganja finally succumbed to jibes against her character from Bianca Del Rio in an unparalleled meltdown in the Untucked lounge.

SEASON 7: "IS THERE SOMETHING ON MY FACE?"

In a stand-off that allegedly went for more than 30 minutes, the so-called sleepy queen Pearl found her self face to face to with an icy Mama Ru after the Supermodel of the World suggested that Pearl had zero personality. The retort that was heard in gay bars across the world – "Is there something on my face?" – woke Pearl up and rebooted her defiant race to the top three.

SEASON 8: "KIMONO-SHE-BETTER-DON'T"

In what could have been the most iconic main stage presentation to date, the Madonna runway was overrun with not one, nor two interpretations of the Queen of Pop's "Nothing Really Matters" kimono look – but four kimonos worn by Derrick Barry, Kim Chi, Naomi Smalls and Thorgy Thor. For a woman with countless iconic and groundbreaking reinventions, how is it that the kimono was all that these queens could conjure up to tribute Madonna?

SEASON 9: "I'D LIKE TO KEEP IT ON PLEASE"

If you're going to wear a mask, how is Ru meant to see your lips move? RuPaul thought Valentina had the chops to go all the way, but it was overconfidence that brought her telenovela story to a crashing end – all to the soundtrack of Ariana Grande's "Greedy". If you're not learning your lyrics, you are not doing drag!

SEASON 10: "FLY FLY FLY FLY... UH OH... UH OH..."

In an attempt to eclipse Sasha Velour's rose petal reveal from Season 9's finale, Asia O'Hara's ill-fated butterfly reveal during her Lip Sync for the Crown against Kameron Michaels showed that tricks are all well and good in theory, but drag and insects just do not mix. Season 10 was just a little bit too extra with those reveals.

ALL STARS SEASON 1: "THE ULTIMATE SHADE OF IT ALL!"

What was expected to be one of the most epic seasons ever with the strongest cast of legendary children of the *Race*, was immediately rocked with the revelation that the queens would compete in teams. Some teams like Chad Michaels and Shannel were perfectly paired to reach the crown, but others found friction, such as Pandora Boxx and Mimi Imfurst who couldn't get their opposites to attract.

ALL STARS SEASON 2: "YOU'RE THAT GIRL I KNEW YOU WERE"

The face crack of the millennium belongs to Phi Phi O'Hara when she was face to face – via a two-way mirror reveal that no one ever saw coming – with Alyssa Edwards as she read Alyssa for her "sloppy" runway presentations and the leniency granted to her by the judges. Despite trying to reinvent her villainous character from Season 4, Phi Phi found herself in the sights of Alyssa (and her camera dress) as she was dressed down for reading Alyssa behind her back... well, in front of her, behind a magic mirror.

ALL STARS SEASON 3: "I'M GOING HOME"

After five maxi challenge wins – the strongest of any *Drag Race* contestant to date – and winning the public's adoration in *All Stars* Season 3, BenDeLaCreme suddenly called it quits after the "Kitty Girls" super group challenge. Wite-Out in hand (courtesy of Thorgy Thor) and head held high, DeLa went home her own kind of winner, without having to play into the season's cut-throat *Survivor*-like format.

ALL STARS SEASON 4: "LIFE'S NOT FAIR!"

Naomi Smalls managed to crush the dreams of both Manila Luzon and fans alike when she called Luzon's name after her falter in the "RuPaul's Best Judy's Race" makeover challenge. The goop of this *All Stars* season proved that when the claws are out, track records are out the window!

RuPaul's Best Friend Race

RAVEN (S02) & JUJUBEE (S02):
The first iconic *Drag Race* friendship of Raven and Jujubee (or Rujubee as we came to call the pair after *All Stars* 1) has seen these queens work and throw shade side by side in programs like *Drag U* and *Drag My Dinner Party* as well as tour the world as a double act treating audiences to both their solo performances and now iconic duet performance of "Dancing on My Own" by Robyn.

THE HEATHERS: RAJA (S03), MANILA LUZON (S03), CARMEN CARRERA (S03) AND DELTA WORK (S03):
Season 3's Heathers have not only toured the world with each other, promoting their single "Lady Marmalade" and shared booths at RuPaul's DragCon, but they've continued to appear on screen together in episodes of *Fashion Photo RuView* serving up equal doses of shade and fierce drag fashion critique.

WILLAM (S04), ALASKA (S05) AND COURTNEY ACT (S06):
Forming the all-powerful Ru-Girl group AAA Girls, Willam, Alaska and Courtney have capitalised on their singing talents to form a super group that has released hit after hit single, which culminated in their debut record and a full-blown choreographed tour of the United States in 2017.

FAME (S07) & VIOLET CHACHKI (S07):
In addition to releasing a single together ("I Run the Runway") the #FashionWives from Season 7 have stormed fashion shows across the globe, have been snapped in full glamour attending New York Fashion Week and even starred in a Pat McGrath Labs promotional video for the makeup giant's range at Sephora in 2017.

TRIXIE MATTEL (S07) & KATYA (S07):
While Trixie and Katya may not have been the dynamic duo we now know and love back in Season 7, these All Stars have eclipsed their runs on *Drag Race* with their very own web series *UNHhhh*, and their Viceland television show *The Trixie & Katya Show*, bringing their brand of offbeat and she-larious senses of humour to audiences the world over.

KIM CHI (S08) & NAOMI SMALLS (S08):
During Season 8 Kim and Naomi slayed the runway with their iconic outfits and makeup looks, which launched their own web series *M.U.G.* (Make Up Girls) critiquing *Drag Race* alumni's makeup artistry and offering real-life makeup hints and tricks to budding drag queens.

Families Who Drag Together

DRAG MOTHERS & DAUGHTERS:

Nicole Paige Brooks (S02) to Phoenix (S03)

Darienne Lake (S06) to Pandora Boxx (S02)
& Mrs. Kasha Davis (S07)

Madame LaQueer (S04) to Lineysha Sparx (S05)

Chad Michaels (S04) to Morgan McMichaels (S02)

Alyssa Edwards (S05) to Shangela (S02/S03)
& Laganja Estranja (S06)

Dax ExclamationPoint (S08) to Violet Chachki (S07)

Sharon Needles (S04) to Aquaria (S10)

Asia O'Hara (S09) to Phi Phi O'Hara (S04)

Bob the Drag Queen (S08) to Miz Cracker (S10)

Alexis Mateo (S03) to Vanessa Vanjie Mateo (S10)

DRAG SISTERS:

Sahara Davenport (S02) & Kennedy Davenport (S07)

Raven (S02), Delta Work (S03), Detox (S05), Mayhem
Miller (S10) & Morgan McMichaels (S02)

April Carrión (S06) & Kandy Ho (S07) – "The Doll
House"

Bob the Drag Queen (S08) & Monét X Change (S10)

Alexis Michelle (S09) & Dusty Ray Bottoms (S10)

QUE

Acid Betty

"No need to adjust your TV sets. This acid trip is all real."

Quick Stats

DRAG RACE:
Season 8

RANKING:
8th place

SIGNATURE LOOK:
Extraterrestrial Hair Extravaganza Realness

TYPE:
Hybrid Drag Queen

FAN-FAVOURITE PERFORMANCE:
"Ruthless" by Acid Betty

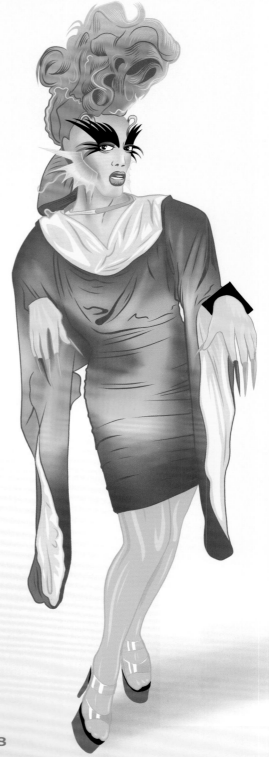

What's the T?

Hailing from Brooklyn, New York, Acid Betty (Jamin Ruhren) started her drag takeover in 2005 in response to her disillusion with the traditional underground drag scene. In the decade predicating her appearance on Season 8 of *Drag Race*, Acid Betty's notoriety in the New York drag scene ascended as she pushed the edges of style, makeup and hair artistry to become a legend of the alternative drag scene. Work with Cazwell and an appearance on *Project Runway* brought Acid Betty's artistry to the public eye, but her appearance on *Drag Race* opened the world up to the out-of-this-world genius with killer punk and alien-esque looks slaying the main stage.

Adore Delano

"I'm not polished enough? I'm polish remover, bitch!"

Quick Stats

DRAG RACES:
Season 6 | *All Stars* 2

RANKING:
Co-runner Up | 9th place

POST DRAG RACE:
Released albums *Till Death Do Us Party* (charted at #59 on the US Billboard 200 chart), *After Party* (#1 US Dance/Electronic chart) and *Whatever*; starred in Starbucks' first LGBT advertisement with Bianca Del Rio

SIGNATURE LOOK:
Band T-shirt and Combat Boots Realness

TYPE:
The Diamond in the Rough

FAN-FAVOURITE PERFORMANCE:
"Patron Tequila" by Paradiso Girls ft. Lil Jon

What's the T?

A seasoned reality TV competitor, Danny Noriega made it as far as the semi-finals on the seventh season of *American Idol* in 2008 before unleashing persona Adore Delano, his YouTube drag character, in 2009. Adore was the perfect blend of Noriega's fiery pop rock sensibility and his mother's so-called "ex-chola" attitude. In the lead-up to her appearance on *RuPaul's Drag Race* in 2014 Adore, inspired by hostess and *Drag Race* royalty Raven, competed and won her first drag contest at Micky's in West Hollywood in 2011.

Competing in the *Race* was a challenge for the green Delano, who fought hard to shake off the criticisms of her sloppy performance and aesthetic. She triumphed in "Shade: The Rusical" and the "Oh No She Betta Don't" rap challenge as well as in the fragrance advertisement challenge alongside drag sister Laganja Estranja, harnessing her personality and charm to forward her way into the top three of the contest. Although finishing as a co-runner up with Courtney Act, Adore won the hearts of the *Drag Race* audience and took control of the second phase of her plan to take over the world.

Releasing her debut album *Till Death Do Us Party* soon after the conclusion of Season 6, Adore Delano went on tour to promote the album across the world. Truly a cross-over star, Delano's album charted higher than any other contestant's releases on the American charts and she has created numerous music videos for the singles, including "I Look Fuckin' Cool" starring Alaska and Nina Flowers. In 2016 Adore competed as a fan-favourite in the second season of *All Stars* where her aesthetic was once again criticised by Michelle Visage, resulting in her decision to tap out of the competition in its second week.

Aja

"You're perfect, you're beautiful, you look like Linda Evangelista..."

Quick Stats

DRAG RACES:
Season 9 | *All Stars* 3

RANKING:
9th place | 7th place

SIGNATURE LOOK:
Urban Female Alien Warrior Realness

TYPE:
The Anime Queen

**FAN-FAVOURITE
PERFORMANCE:**
"Glass & Patron" by FKA Twigs

What's the T?

A young Brooklyn legend in the making, Aja (Jay Rivera) began playing with drag at the age of 16, inspired by the big city around her and the strong imagery of anime girls and super villains. A fan-favourite from the outset, Aja's personal development in her short run on Season 9 of *Drag Race* was as exciting to watch as her head-turning runway presentations. Returning to screens in the third season of *All Stars*, Aja death dropped from new heights, showcasing her evolved aesthetic and applying her growth to her kawaii ghetto main stage attire (including a sickening Princess Disastah RuDemption Runway!) and "Snatch Game" performance as Crystal LaBeija. Unleashing her debut EP *In My Feelings* in 2018 to a whole new world of rap fans, Aja continues to slay as head of the Haus of Aja drag collective back in New York City.

AJA

Akashia

"Every competition needs a bitch, and that bitch is ME and I'm happy with that."

Quick Stats

DRAG RACE:
Season 1

RANKING:
7th place

SIGNATURE LOOK:
Sassy Streetwalker Realness

TYPE:
Sickening Stripper Queen

FAN-FAVOURITE PERFORMANCE:
"Bring Me to Life" by Evanescence

What's the T?

Inspired by the movie *Queen of the Damned*, Akashia (Eric Flint) from Cleveland, Ohio, ascended from local performances to drag fame after appearing on Season 1 of *Drag Race*, flaunting her sass and her ass as one of the very first "body queens" on the show. Famous for both her slip on the main stage and her epic lip sync against Tammie Brown to Michelle Williams' "We Break the Dawn", Akashia continues to entertain in nightclubs across the United States, leaving the crowds always wanting more.

SHIA

Alaska

"Hieeee!"

Quick Stats

DRAG RACES:
Season 5 | *All Stars* 2

RANKING:
Co-runner Up | Winner

POST DRAG RACE:
Stars in WOW-produced web series
Bro'Laska with her brother Cory
Binney; released records *Anus* (2015),
Poundcake (2016), *Access All Areas*
with Willam and Courtney Act (2016),
and *Amethyst Journey* with Jeremy
Mikush (2018); created and released
her very own Lil' Poundcake talking
doll!; appeared in Little Mix's music
video for "Power" (2017)

SIGNATURE LOOK:
Tacky Blonde Bombshell Realness

TYPE:
The Trash to Treasure Queen

**FAN-FAVOURITE
PERFORMANCE:**
"Hieeee" by Alaska

What's the T?

Alaska Thunderfuck 5000 (Justin Honard) cut his teeth as a drag queen in 2009 at Fubar in West Hollywood after a departure from acting. Hailing from Pittsburgh, Alaska returned to her hometown in 2010 to pursue both a drag career and a relationship with Sharon Needles with whom she formed the band Haus of Haunt. Inspired by "tranimal" and other non-conformist styles of drag, Alaska was the perfect blend of trash and glamour and drew the attention of fans for many years prior to her appearance on *Drag Race*.

Following the win of then-partner Sharon Needles, Alaska powered through Season 5 notoriously never having to lip sync for her life, just like Season 2 winner Tyra Sanchez. Winning the "Sugar Ball" and "Scent of a Drag Queen" challenges late in the contest solidified Alaska's brand of trash-glamour as well as her raunchy sense of humour that garnered wide adoration from viewers of the competition; fans were tickled pink by her *Red for Filth*. Although she was co-runner up with Florida powerhouse Roxxxy Andrews to Jinkx Monsoon, Alaska was able to shake off the label of "Sharon's Boyfriend" and began the road to becoming what Willam has described as "The Future of Drag".

Alaska was called back to compete in the second season of *All Stars* in 2016, where she proved through winning four main challenges and performing epic lip syncs for her legacy, that she deserved her place in the Drag Race Hall of Fame alongside *All Stars* Season 1 winner Chad Michaels.

Alaska has appeared on stage in *The Rocky Horror Show*, *Sex and the City* and her own show *Red for Filth* as well as becoming one of the leading fully fledged drag recording artists. After being cast as a spokesmodel in a 2014 American Apparel campaign, Alaska joined forced with her fellow AAA Girls Willam and Courtney Act to embark on a musical collaboration and release their drag girl-group debut record. In 2018 Alaska and Willam continued their creative partnership with their very first podcast series *Race Chaser*, which dissects every episode of *Drag Race* all the way from Season 1 Episode 1.

Alexis Mateo

"BAM!"

Quick Stats

DRAG RACES:
Season 3 | *All Stars* 1

RANKING:
3rd place | 5th/6th place

SIGNATURE LOOK:
Latina Princess Realness

TYPE:
Puerto Rican Pageant Queen

**FAN-FAVOURITE
PERFORMANCE:**
"A Woman's Drag (Joelapuss Remix)"
by Various

What's the T?

A seasoned pageant queen direct from Puerto Rico via Florida, Alexis Mateo (Alexis Mateo Pacheco) has been crowned numerous titles including Miss Florida USofA and All American Goddess 2016 since commencing her drag career in 2001. After successfully reaching the top three in Season 3 of *Drag Race*, famously winning the military P.S.A. challenge, Alexis went on to compete alongside fellow Puerto Rican goddess Yara Sofia in the first *All Stars* season, where she took the catchphrases, laughs and wacky hair extravaganzas audiences love about her and turned it up to 100!

LEXIS
ATEO

Alexis Michelle

"If you see something, say something."

Quick Stats

DRAG RACE:
Season 9

RANKING:
5th place

SIGNATURE LOOK:
Curve, Swerve and Cinch Realness

TYPE:
The Theatre Queen

FAN–FAVOURITE PERFORMANCE:
"Into the Woods (Live) /Gorgeous Medley" by Barbara Harris

What's the T?

A drag pro of over 15 years and lover of all things musical theatre, New York's Alexis Michelle (Alex Michaels) had won fans all over the world wide web with her *So You Think You Can Drag?* competition-winning performances before appearing on Season 9 of *Drag Race*. Having auditioned eight times prior to her casting, Alexis entered the *Race* as an all-singing all-swinging kinda queen with a strong performing bone and a super-polished mug. While Alexis' runway presentations didn't always win the judges' applause – Lady Gaga did love her Versace-inspired gown! – she delivered show-stealing performances in "Kardashian: The Musical" as Kris Jenner and in the "Snatch Game", where she took the challenge win for her impersonation of Liza Minnelli. Faced with the challenge of serving three fashion-forward runway looks in the "Gayest Ball Ever", Alexis stumbled with her Village People Eleganza Extravaganza and was sent packing to the tune of "Macho Man" by Peppermint. Following her time on Season 9, Alexis has not only released a bitch house track with fellow Racers Aja, Peppermint and Sasha Velour entitled "C.L.A.T.", but her own debut record "Lovefool" on Broadway Records in 2018.

Bar Queen

A drag queen who makes an effort to get-up in drag but may not be one of the performers on stage – or necessarily even want to be a showgirl. Instead, she spends a lot of her time at the bar being a social butterfly. Tatianna was referred to as a "bar queen" by Shannel in Season 1 of *All Stars*, suggesting that she was hardly in the same league as the drag queens in that season.

Beat

A queen's beat is the makeup and lashes that are applied to create the glamazon illusion. A truly "beat face" is a face of makeup that is so strong that the queen would be considered stunning or "beat for the gods" (see also: "For the Gods"). The term can also be used as a way to describe the process of making over the face. For example: "Valentina beat her face real good tonight!".

Alisa Summers

"I'm definitely a fishy queen. I can walk down the street and I can never get clocked!"

Quick Stats

DRAG RACE:
Season 4

RANKING:
13th place

SIGNATURE LOOK:
Futuristic Fantasy Fish Realness

TYPE:
Sequinned Show Queen

FAN-FAVOURITE PERFORMANCE:
"Finally" by CeCe Peniston

What's the T?

Coming from a strong Florida drag family background and wins in the pageant scene, Alisa Summers (Alex Hernandez) competed in Season 4 of *Drag Race* with good performance experience behind her. After failing to create a memorable post-apocalyptic couture look on the runway, Alisa (and her breastplate) lost in a lip sync battle against Jiggly Caliente (and her baked potato couture). Since her time on *Drag Race*, Alisa Summers has continued to strut her stuff on stage in Tampa, Florida to clamouring fans.

Alyssa Edwards

"Every woman has a secret. Mine happens to be a little bigger."

Quick Stats

DRAG RACES:
Season 5 | *All Stars* 2

RANKING:
6th place | 5th place (originally 6th)

POST DRAG RACE:
Starred in her very own World of Wonder web series *Alyssa's Secret*; continues to direct her Texas-based dance company Beyond Belief; choreographed and performed with pop star Miley Cyrus at the 2015 MTV Video Music Awards; starred in her own Netflix documentary series *Dancing Queen*

SIGNATURE LOOK:
Miss America Realness

TYPE:
The Dancing Queen

FAN-FAVOURITE PERFORMANCE:
"Indestructible Medley" by Various Artists

What's the T?

A long-time competitor in the drag pageantry circuit, Alyssa Edwards (Justin Johnson) competed and won numerous pageant titles including Miss Gay Texas America 2004–2005, Miss Gay USofA 2006 and All American Goddess 2010. A dancing queen and fierce performer from Mesquite, Texas, Alyssa appeared in the 2008 documentary *Pageant* and built her Beyond Belief Dance Company prior to her appearance on *RuPaul's Drag Race*.

Emerging as one of the most well-rounded performance queens in *Drag Race* herstory, Alyssa Edwards was immediately positioned as the nemesis of fellow contestant Coco Montrese with whom she shared the history of pageant dethroning and title stripping. The history of these two contestants reared its head throughout Season 5, culminating in an epic Lip Sync for Your Life to Paula Abdul's "Cold Hearted" where Edwards was ultimately out-performed by her pageant sister. Prior to her elimination Alyssa became one hell of a quotable queen, melding her southern charm with old school catchphrases to create memorable lines such as "Backrolls!?", "Get a grip, get a life and get over it" and "I don't get cute, I get drop dead gorgeous".

In 2016, Alyssa returned to prime time television, guns blazing, with her appearance on *All Stars* 2 where she went on to win two main challenges and solidify her status as a legendary icon of the *Race*.

Winning a new legion of fans from the show, Alyssa talks wigs, nails and dating in drag in her web series *Alyssa's Secret* and, as a fashionista, Edwards has graced the LA Fashion Week Marco Marco runway on multiple occasions. In 2018 Alyssa Edward's very first Netflix documentary series *Dancing Queen* was released, chronicling her day to day experiences as a drag queen by night and dance teacher by day, and showcasing the Beyond Belief Dance Company.

April Carrión

"Ay Dios Mio!"

Quick Stats

DRAG RACE:
Season 6

RANKING:
11th place

SIGNATURE LOOK:
April Showers Realness

TYPE:
Art-School Androgyny Queen

**FAN-FAVOURITE
PERFORMANCE:**
"Slow" by Kylie Minogue

What's the T?

Excelling as an arts college student, Puerto Rico's April Carrión (Jason Carrión) joined the Season 6 cast of *Drag Race* inspired by both the glamour and androgyny of previous contestant Nina Flowers. Following her time on the *Race*, where she served colourful and creative costumes on the runway, April has continued performing and modelling in drag and has also gone on to produce the documentary *Mala Mala*, which explores the lives of drag queens and young transgender people in Puerto Rico.

Aquaria

"Bonjour!"

Quick Stats

DRAG RACE:
Season 10

RANKING:
Winner

SIGNATURE LOOK:
Starry Eyed Club-Kid Realness

TYPE:
The Social Media Superstar

**FAN-FAVOURITE
PERFORMANCE:**
"Werq the World Medley" by Various

What's the T?

A Pennsylvanian-born fashion student with a background in dance, Aquaria (Giovanni Palandrani) experimented with the art of drag in high school, counting *Drag Race* winner Sharon Needles as her drag mentor, who would sneak her into gay clubs to soak up the formula to become the next drag sensation. A social media star from early on in her career, Aquaria found fame as a punky club-kid within the ranks of Susanne Bartsch's party scene in New York City long before ever appearing on *Drag Race*, appearing with Bartsch and Sasha Velour in a *Vogue Italia* spread in 2016. With fashion heavyweights like Jeremy Scott joining hundreds of thousands of Instagram fans in their collective excitement for Aquaria's appearance on *Drag Race*, it's safe to say the world was waiting with bated breath for this stylish young queen to slay. And slay Aquaria did in Season 10 of *Drag Race*, delivering, as RuPaul said, some of the most iconic fashion moments since legends like Raja and Detox, winning the "Evil Twins" and "Last Ball on Earth" costuming challenges. Showing that her comedy skills are as honed as her style eye, Aquaria took home the win for the "Snatch Game" as Melania Trump before powering her way to winning the crown, having not ever fallen into the bottom two. Aquaria's worldwide takeover since Season 10 has seen her rack up over 28 million views for her *Vogue* and *Cosmopolitan* makeover videos, release the single "Burn Rubber" (2018) and tour every corner of the globe. Predestined for greatness by the stars, Aquaria truly is a queen for the modern era – "I don't define drag, drag is defined by me".

Asia O'Hara

"It's about to be Asia O'Hara's Drag Race! I'm about to own this whole building!"

Quick Stats

DRAG RACE:
Season 10

RANKING:
4th place

SIGNATURE LOOK:
Tweety Bird Eleganza

TYPE:
The Supreme Pageant Queen

FAN-FAVOURITE PERFORMANCE:
"Neon Lights Medley" by Various

What's the T?

A legendary queen in her own right, Asia O'Hara (Antwan Mason Lee) from Dallas, Texas sports a drag résumé that leaves others in her dust. Crowned Miss Gay USofA 2007, All American Goddess 2012 and Miss Gay America 2016, this national title champion started her career in 2003 and is an accomplished costume designer, dance and colour guard instructor. Coming from a long line of O'Hara pageant divas – she's drag mother to Season 4's Phi Phi O'Hara – Asia is one of the most accomplished queens to ever enter *RuPaul's Drag Race*. With expectations high and fellow competitors quaking in their heels, Asia did not disappoint as she powered through the competition to the finale, winning the "Tap That App" and "Breastworld" comedy challenges and serving up some of the most elaborate costumes (that dandelion look!) ever seen on the main stage. Met with an unlikely fluttering foe or fifty at the finale, Asia O'Hara's butterfly reveal act in the Lip Sync for Your Legacy against Kameron Michaels fell flat, landing her in fourth place and subsequently sparked mild backlash against her decision to use live creatures. While her *Drag Race* crown wasn't awarded this time around, Asia has been able to tour her high-energy act across the world and has even released her first dance single "Queen for Tonight". If there's a queen begging to return for *All Stars* one day it's Asia!

BeBe Zahara Benet

"Rrrrra-ka-ta-ti-ti-ta-ta, Yeah, I'm pussy, bitch!"

Quick Stats

DRAG RACES:
Season 1 | *All Stars* 3

RANKING:
Winner | 3rd/4th place

POST DRAG RACE:
Released several dance singles on iTunes including "I'm the Shit" (2009), "Cameroon" (2010) and "Jungle Kitty" (2018); fierce Drag Professor at *RuPaul's Drag U*; makes appearances across the United States as a public speaker on pride, drag and the effect of her West African upbringing

SIGNATURE LOOK:
African Animal Skin Realness

TYPE:
The Cameroonian Goddess

FAN-FAVOURITE PERFORMANCE:
"Miss USofA 2005 Medley" by Various Artists

What's the T?

Hailing from Cameroon, Nea Marshall Kudi Ngwa worked as a male model in Paris and had his first taste of drag after filling in after an unexpected no-show of a female model. BeBe Zahara Benet was born out of that gender-bending runway moment. She saw herself as a "strong and cunty character illusion created for entertainment and the artistic expression of the feminine psyche". Emerging from the Minneapolis drag scene, BeBe starred in the very first season of *RuPaul's Drag Race*, bringing a sense of international influence and worldly aesthetic to the competition. Winning two main challenges, she was one of the strongest competitors, only having to lip sync for her life in a wig-throwing showdown against Ongina to Britney Spears' "Stronger".

Always poised, softly spoken and serving face, BeBe Zahara Benet snatched the crown from runners up Nina Flowers and Rebecca Glasscock after an iconic appearance in the first *Drag Race* music video for "Cover Girl". After her triumphant win in the first season of *Drag Race*, BeBe went on to create a theatre piece called *Queendom* where she incorporated live original music that fused pop music with African rhythms, elaborate costuming, live singers and dance elements.

The Jungle Kitty returned in *All Stars* Season 3 as the surprise 10th contestant. BeBe showcased to a whole new audience (in HD!) just why RuPaul crowned the OG back in 2009, with her wins of the "Pop Art Ball" and "Handmaids to Kitty Girls" challenges, pushing her all the way to the top 4 – rrrrra-ka-ta-ti-ti-ta-ta!

BenDeLa-Creme

"DeLa for short. De for shorter. Ms Creme if you're nasty."

Quick Stats

DRAG RACES:
Season 6 | *All Stars* 3

RANKING:
5th place (Miss Congeniality) | 6th place

POST DRAG RACE:
Produced critically acclaimed solo shows *Terminally Delightful*, *Cosmos* and *Inferno A-Go-Go*; curated her own line of cruelty-free cosmetics and fragrance ("Candy from a Baby") with Atomic Cosmetics

SIGNATURE LOOK:
Kitsch Housewife Realness

TYPE:
The Character Queen

FAN-FAVOURITE PERFORMANCE:
"The Little Mermaid Medley" from *The Little Mermaid Original Soundtrack*

What's the T?

While pursuing a Bachelor of Fine Arts at the School of the Art Institute of Chicago, the now Seattle-based Benjamin Putnam started his drag career in 2002 as BenDeLaCreme. A terminally delightful drag queen housewife, DeLa's inherently political show sensibility reflected her upbringing within the drag king scene of Chicago. Following her move to Seattle, she ran DeLouRue Presents, a theatrical production company producing work featuring both drag and burlesque acts, notably Season 5 winner Jinkx Monsoon. Prior to her appearance on *Drag Race*, DeLa also appeared on screen in the documentary film *Waxie Moon* by Wes Hurley.

Miss Congeniality of Season 6 of *RuPaul's Drag Race*, BenDeLaCreme demonstrated exceptional sewing, comedic, musical and impersonation skills throughout the contest. Although winner of the fan-favourite "Snatch Game", portraying actress Maggie Smith in her role from *Downton Abbey*, DeLa fought off stiff criticism from the judges that she hid behind character facades. In a *Drag Race* first, BenDeLaCreme lip synced for her life on two separate controversial occasions against Darienne Lake, ultimately missing out on making the top four of the contest. Joining the cast of *All Stars* 3, BenDeLaCreme became the very first contestant in *Drag Race* herstory to win five maxi challenges as she delivered iconic performances in both comedic and creative challenges. On track to win the whole competition, BenDeLaCreme shook audiences the world over as she eliminated herself after winning the "Handmaids to Kitty Girls" challenge, leaving on her own terms as a champion. Since her appearances on *Drag Race*, DeLa has continued to tour the world and produce and perform in theatre shows, including the critically acclaimed *Inferno A-Go-Go* and *Drag Becomes Her*, alongside Jinkx Monsoon and Peaches Christ.

DRAG TERM

Booger

A drag queen who is considered inept or lazy
in their drag artistry. Booger drag can also
describe an aesthetic style pertaining to poorly
chosen outfits, bad makeup application or sloppy
performance on stage.

DRAG TERM

Busted

Similar to "booger", "busted" is a way to describe a queen as either very ugly or poorly put together.

Bianca Del Rio

"My style is very Joan Crawford/Bozo the Clown. It's versatile... I'm not, but the look is."

Quick Stats

DRAG RACE:
Season 6

RANKING:
Winner

POST DRAG RACE:
Starred in her own comedy films *Hurricane Bianca* (2016) and *Hurricane Bianca 2: from Russia with Hate* (2018); appeared alongside Adore Delano in a Starbucks coffee campaign; performed at the 2015 Vienna Life Ball alongside Courtney Act and Eurovision's Conchita Wurst

SIGNATURE LOOK:
Old Hollywood Meets Clown Realness

TYPE:
The Stand-Up Comedian

FAN-FAVOURITE PERFORMANCE:
"Palladio" by Escala AKA "Bianca Del Rio Makes a Dress on Stage"

What's the T?

Hailing from Gretna, Louisiana, Roy Haylock started his drag artistry in 1996 after working for many years as a costume designer. Emerging as Bianca Del Rio, the sharp-tongued New Orleans Gay Entertainer of the Year performed regularly before moving to New York after Hurricane Katrina. Prior to appearing on *Drag Race*, Del Rio established herself as one of the most iconic drag performers in the US alongside other icons Linda Simpson, Lady Bunny, Sherry Vine and Hedda Lettuce. The latter three were featured alongside Bianca in the web series *Queens of Drag: NYC* in 2010, who also performed in the comedy special *One Night Stand Up: Dragtastic! NYC* on Logo TV.

After pressure from her peers and her own drive to "show 'em how it's done", Bianca Del Rio was cast in *RuPaul's Drag Race*. The immediate front runner and fan-favourite for her quick wit, strong performance in all aspects of the competition and "Mama Bear" disposition, Del Rio won three main challenges before taking out the crown of America's Next Drag Superstar. Fans' unwavering support for Bianca's stinging sense of humour saw her debut film project *Hurricane Bianca* gain successful crowd-funding and was released in 2016, starring *Drag Race* alumni Joslyn Fox, Willam, Shangela and Alyssa Edwards. A sequel – *Hurricane Bianca 2: From Russia with Hate* – was released in 2018. In the years after *Drag Race*, Bianca has successfully toured her comedy shows *Rolodex of Hate*, *Not Today Satan* and *Blame It on Bianca Del Rio*, spreading her brand of poison-tongued hilarity across the world.

Blair St. Clair

"I do declare, I am the Blair St. Clair, and I'm coming out!"

Quick Stats

DRAG RACE:
Season 10

RANKING:
9th place

SIGNATURE LOOK:
Silver Screen Glamour

TYPE:
The Southern Sweetheart

FAN-FAVOURITE PERFORMANCE:
"Now or Never" by Blair St. Clair

What's the T?

Introduced to the world of drag after landing a role as Mercedes in *La Cage Aux Folles* in 2014, Indiana's Blair St. Clair (Andrew Bryson) fell in love with the art of female illusion and musical performance. Aware that Indiana's drag scene called for excellence, Blair went on to win the prestigious pageant title of Miss Gay Indiana 2016, all the while pursuing a theatre career as an actor. With acting and singing chops to rival the greatest broadway queens of the *Race*, Blair walked into the Season 10 werkroom delivering show tune sass ready to show she's more than just a pretty face. Placing high in her first three challenges and delivering runways giving nods to old Hollywood, it was after a heartfelt performance of Diana Ross' "I'm Coming Out" against The Vixen when Blair St. Clair had to bid her castmates farewell. Blair's elimination revelation that she was sexually assaulted, has enabled her to speak on this topic extensively in her time after *Drag Race*, addressing to a wider audience the reality of sexual assault amongst men in college settings. A phoenix rising, Blair is ready for the next steps in her drag career, releasing two singles (with *Drag Race* star-studded music videos) "Now or Never" and "Call My Life" in 2018.

Bob the Drag Queen

"Purse first! Purse first! Walk into the room purse first!"

Quick Stats

DRAG RACE:
Season 8

RANKING:
Winner

SIGNATURE LOOK:
Banjee Glam Realness

TYPE:
The People's Queen

FAN-FAVOURITE PERFORMANCE:
"Crazy" by Gnarls Barkley

What's the T?

Inspired by the first season of *Drag Race*, Bob the Drag Queen (Christopher Caldwell) honed her skills in New York City as a quick-witted and politically aware stand-up queen of comedy for over several years before being cast on *RuPaul's Drag Race*. Excelling in costume creation challenges and bringing out two fully realised polar opposite "Snatch Game" characters (Uzo Aduba and Carol Channing), Bob harnessed her confidence and cheeky honesty to win over audiences and RuPaul to be crowned the eighth winner of the *Race*. Bob's iconic "purse first" entrance onto the main stage has led to a successful club single of the same name and a social media meme explosion. Since the *Race*, fans continue to get their fix of Bob's comedy stylings on the Viceland program *The Trixie & Katya Show* (filling in for Katya), on Bob's own Logo TV comedy special *Suspiciously Large Woman* (2017) and in podcast/web series *Sibling Rivalry* with Season 10 sister Monét X Change.

Carmen Carrera

"If you find a flaw, let me know."

Quick Stats

DRAG RACE:
Season 3

RANKING:
5th place (originally 6th)

POST DRAG RACE:
Featured on the fifth anniversary cover of *C*NDY* magazine along with 13 other transgender women including Laverne Cox and Janet Mock; poster girl for the 2014 Life Ball in Vienna shot by David LaChapelle; starred in "Showgirl!" – a Steven Meisel *W* magazine shoot and promo video; petitioned to be a 2013 Victoria's Secret Fashion Show model

SIGNATURE LOOK:
Bulletproof Body Realness

TYPE:
The Jersey Showgirl

FAN-FAVOURITE PERFORMANCE:
"I Am the Body Beautiful" by Salt-N-Pepa

What's the T?

Starting her drag career in the mid 2000s, New Jersey's Carmen Carrera (Carmen Roman) started performing at legendary Latino showgirl club La Escuelita in the heart of Manhattan. Many years prior to her transition into the beautiful transgender woman she is today, Carrera dealt with her sexuality and understanding of gender through honing her craft as a burlesque drag performer with the support of trans drag mother Angela Carrera. Improving her sex kitten act over the years, Carmen increased her bookings and went on to play The Polo Club in Hartford, meeting *Drag Race* alumni Manila Luzon and Sahara Davenport along the way.

Carrera was cast in the third season of *RuPaul's Drag Race* and became very well known for her perfect proportions and buxom booty, as critiqued by Jersey girl Michelle Visage as a crutch – "Stop relying on that body!". Though wowing audiences with countless almost-nude runway presentations, Carmen – a member of the Heathers clique – didn't win any major challenges and was eliminated twice after being brought back by the judges for a second chance at the crown.

Carrera commenced her transition soon after taping *Drag Race* in 2010. Her flawless looks drew the eye of renowned fashion photographer Steven Meisel, who had Carmen star in his "Showgirl" *W* magazine and video shoot.

Carrera has become a trans role model, starring on occasion with television star Laverne Cox, in various reality programs addressing transphobia in the wider community and slaying catwalks across the United States.

Chad Michaels

"Everything I've gone through has been because of Cher."

Quick Stats

DRAG RACES:
Season 4 | *All Stars* 1

RANKING:
Co-runner Up | Winner

POST DRAG RACE:
Starred in CW's *Jane the Virgin*;
opened for Cher at the launch of her
"Woman's World" single; released
single "Tragic Girl" (2013) with
Liquid360

SIGNATURE LOOK:
Polished Drag Mother Realness

TYPE:
The Drag Assassin

**FAN-FAVOURITE
PERFORMANCE:**
"EOY (Entertainer of the Year) 2010
Medley" by Cher

What's the T?

With over 20 years of experience as a drag performer, Chad Michaels is the definition of an All Star and an icon – much like her own idol, Cher. Drag daughter to the legendary Hunter, Michaels hails from San Diego and has performed as one of, if not the premier, Cher impersonators in the world. Impersonation of the original diva has seen Chad entertain clubs across the US, on Las Vegas stages and has given her the opportunity to perform for industry favourites such as Elton John, Christina Aguilera and Cher herself.

Entering the fourth season of the *Race* as a seasoned professional, Chad Michaels was not only miles ahead of her competition in her understanding and execution of her drag skills but she set the bar for characterisation and polish. Although winning the "Snatch Game" as Cher and giving memorable performances throughout the season, Chad finished as co-runner up with Phi Phi O'Hara. Chad's loss of the crown didn't last long as she was soon snatched up to compete in the first season of *All Stars* in which she took the crown and the first position in the RuPaul's Drag Race Hall of Fame.

Following her performance in both Season 4 and *All Stars*, Chad Michaels continues to produce and perform in the *Dreamgirls Revue*, sharing the stage with, among others, Delta Work, Jasmine Masters and her drag daughter Morgan McMichaels. A master of impersonation, Chad constantly reinvents her drag and her repertoire of characters with old-school diva Bette Davis and new-school icon Lady Gaga.

Charlie
Hides

"Hi, hi, hi! It's about to get shady up in here."

Quick Stats

DRAG RACE:
Season 9

RANKING:
12th place

SIGNATURE LOOK:
Pop-Art Mod Realness

TYPE:
The Transatlantic Dame

**FAN-FAVOURITE
PERFORMANCE:**
"Burlesque Medley" by Cher

What's the T?

A cabaret and cruise liner performer for over 20 years, Boston-via-London's Charlie Hides truly is the godmother of drag and a master of shady impersonation. Through widely popular celebrity impersonation and parody videos on YouTube, Charlie entered *RuPaul's Drag Race* as a fan-favourite with audiences at the ready for her cutting sense of humour and wit – and, of course, that iconic Madonna impersonation in the "Snatch Game".

Unfortunately Charlie Hides' run in the *Race* didn't last long as a stumble in the "Good Morning Bitches!" challenge, combined with a less than mobile lip sync to Britney Spears' "I Wanna Go", saw The Dame go... home. Following *Drag Race*, Charlie has toured her act across the globe and has released the singles "Bitch Thin" (2018) and "The Dame" (2017).

Chi Chi DeVayne

*"I don't get ready – I stay ready!" *finger snap**

Quick Stats

DRAG RACES:
Season 8 | *All Stars* 3

RANKING:
4th place | 8th place

SIGNATURE LOOK:
Southern Belle Realness

TYPE:
Crafty Country Queen

**FAN-FAVOURITE
PERFORMANCE:**
"Emotions" by Mariah Carey

What's the T?

The loveable and self proclaimed "cheap queen" of Louisiana, Chi Chi DeVayne (Zavion Davenport) started her career much like many other queens, with a spur of the moment Halloween dress up... as Nicki Minaj, of course! After years of dancing the house down in the Louisiana drag scene, the high-energy DeVayne was cast in the eighth season of *Drag Race*. Chi Chi's performance in the challenges saw her glide through the competition via an EPIC Lip Sync for Your Life to Jennifer Holliday's "And I Am Telling You I'm Not Going" (in full black and white drag!) to the final episode and a top 4 placing. After winning the hearts of fans following her time on Season 8, Chi Chi was invited back to compete in the third season of *All Stars* where, while her style reigned supreme on the runway, she found the competition a lot harder than her first run in the *Race* and found herself in the bottom three times before being eliminated by Shangela. DeVayne continues to follow her dreams of serving powerful dancing diva ferocity across the globe, slaying the children one city at a time!

Cheesecake

A term to describe a queen with not only a
gorgeous and curvy body, but the ability to sell
her sexiness as well. This was one of DiDa Ritz's
favourite sayings as she entered the werkroom
in Season 4.

DRAG TERM

Clock

To call out a queen's flaw they've been trying
to hide, uncover the truth about a situation or to
reveal a drag queen's true gender, e.g. "The judges
clocked Kandy Ho's beard contour!".

Coco Montrese

"Orange you glad
to see me?"

Quick Stats

DRAG RACES:
Season 5 | *All Stars* 2

RANKING:
5th place | 10th place

SIGNATURE LOOK:
Janet Jackson Realness

TYPE:
The Lip Sync Diva of Las Vegas

**FAN-FAVOURITE
PERFORMANCE:**
"Super Bowl Medley" by Janet Jackson

What's the T?

An icon of the drag pageantry circuit, a former Miss Gay America and Las Vegas legend, Coco Montrese (Martin Cooper) has entertained legions of fans since 1992 not only as Coco but as the world's premier Janet Jackson impersonator. With pageant titles and an incomparable lip syncing ability under her belt, Coco Montrese appeared on the fifth season of *RuPaul's Drag Race* as a contestant-to-beat. Pitted against pageant peer Alyssa Edwards from the outset, Coco proved through three lip syncs for her life and her win of the "RuPaul Roast" that she is strongest on stage entertaining the masses. In the years after her appearance on *Drag Race*, Coco's one-liners and iconic "Tang" highlight have served as fan-favourite memes, leading to her return to screens on the second season of *All Stars* where she was eliminated in the first week of the contest.

Courtney Act

"If everyone else is relying on ugly, why can't I rely on pretty?"

Quick Stats

DRAG RACE:
Season 6

RANKING:
Co-runner Up

POST DRAG RACE:
Became the inaugural Sydney Gay and Lesbian Mardi Gras Official Ambassador in 2014; stars in web series *American Act* for Australian media website Junkee as a comedic US foreign correspondent; appeared in Little Mix's music video for "Power" (2017); won *Celebrity Big Brother* (UK) in 2018; host of E!'s reality dating show *The Bi Life* in 2018.

SIGNATURE LOOK:
Catalogue Model Realness

TYPE:
The Fishy Queen

FAN-FAVOURITE PERFORMANCE:
"Nutbush City Limits" (with Jake Shears at Sydney Mardi Gras) by Ike and Tina Turner

What's the T?

Emerging on Australian screens as both Shane Jenek (real name) and Courtney Act on the first season of *Australian Idol*, Courtney demonstrated her brand of fiery performance and camp sensibility enabling her to make it through to the Wild Card heat of the contest. Act immediately drew the attention of audiences, performing at the Sydney Opera House as part of the finale and touring Australia. Following the release of her debut single "Rub Me Wrong", Courtney became a mainstay on morning television as a featured cosmetics spokesmodel. A big fish in a little pond, Act moved to the US in the early 2010s and became a West Hollywood karaoke hostess and YouTube star.

Courtney was cast in *Drag Race* and was soon seen as a contender for the crown. Despite a rocky reception from judge Michelle Visage who accused Act of "relying on pretty", Courtney delivered countless sickening runway presentations including her take on RuPaul in the iconic Bob Mackie silver gown. Building a friendship with on-screen star Chaz Bono as well as fellow contestants Darienne Lake, Adore Delano and Bianca Del Rio, Act came out as a co-runner up winning the adoration of new fans across the US.

Although she had released pop singles since as early as 2004 in Australia, in 2015 Courtney released her debut EP *Kaleidoscope* and teamed up with her fellow American Apparel Ad girls Willam and Alaska to release a string of cheeky parody singles and even their own album of original and parody material in 2016. Even after a slight costume malfunction, 2018 proved to be the year of Courtney Act as her intelligence and charm won over the British public to earn her the title of *Celebrity Big Brother* winner!

Cynthia Lee Fontaine

"How you doin' Mis Amores? Are you ready to see my cucu, AGAIN?"

Quick Stats

DRAG RACES:
Season 8 | Season 9

RANKING:
10th place (Miss Congeniality) |
10th place

SIGNATURE LOOK:
Glamour Clown Realness

TYPE:
The Puerto Rican Shangela

FAN-FAVOURITE PERFORMANCE:
"I'm Outta Love" by Anastacia

What's the T?

Puerto Rico's Cynthia Lee Fontaine (Carlos Hernandez) enjoyed a successful drag career in Austin, Texas, earning titles such as Miss Texas Continental in 2012 before being cast in Season 8 of *Drag Race*. A fan-favourite despite a short run in the season, Cynthia won audiences over with both her "cucu" and her huge heart to win the title of Miss Congeniality. Amid bringing her brand of effervescent Latina loca to the world, Cynthia Lee Fontaine was diagnosed with stage one liver cancer, slowing down her entertainment schedule. With this in mind, RuPaul decided to give "Miss Cucugeniality" a second chance to prove herself once recovered, in the ninth season of the *Race*, where she brought back the bonkers sense of humour right up until her performance as Sofia Vergara in the "Snatch Game".

Darienne Lake

"Two tons of fun, of twisted steel and sex appeal."

Quick Stats

DRAG RACE:
Season 6

RANKING:
4th place

SIGNATURE LOOK:
Plus-size Pinup Realness

TYPE:
Campy Glamour Queen

FAN-FAVOURITE PERFORMANCE:
"Hello" by Martin Solveig ft. Dragonette

What's the T?

Emerging in August of 1990, Rochester's Miss Darienne Lake (Greg Meyer) has entertained audiences on stage and screen ever since, with club shows as well as appearances on iconic 90s chat shows. Her appearance on *Ricki Lake* with drag daughter and *Drag Race* alum Pandora Boxx in an episode named "Get a grip doll... you're too fat to be a drag queen", demonstrates the brilliantly crazy world of both 90s drag and 90s trash TV! After years of auditioning for *Drag Race*, Darienne Lake finally made the cut in the sixth season where she proved that a big girl can hold her own among the slighter queens, from both a style and comedy angle. Following her top 4 performance on the *Race*, Darienne has toured as part of the Battle of the Seasons Tour and even appeared on the *Christmas Queens* album in 2015 in a group track with Pandora Boxx and fellow New Yorker Ivy Winters.

Dax Exclama-tionpoint

"What's up nerds?"

Quick Stats

DRAG RACE:
Season 8

RANKING:
11th/12th place

SIGNATURE LOOK:
Superhero Showgirl Realness

TYPE:
Cosplay Queen of All Nerds

**FAN-FAVOURITE
PERFORMANCE:**
"Baby's On Fire" by Die Antwoord

What's the T?

A queen with roots in Savannah, Georgia, Dax ExclamationPoint (Dax Martin) began creating her drag persona in response to what she felt was a tired drag scene, harnessing her comic book fandom and club-kid creativity to break the mould. Drag mother to Season 7's winner Violet Chachki, Dax was cast in the eighth season of the *Race* where she excelled in a Hello Kitty costume challenge but gave an unfortunately weak lip sync performance to the iconic "I Will Survive" by Gloria Gaynor against Laila McQueen. Both queens were told to sashay away in the second-ever double elimination on *Drag Race*. Dax continues to bring her brand of exquisitely created superhero and villainess looks to stages across the United States, joining Phi Phi O'Hara as one of *Drag Race*'s premier cosplay queens.

Delta Work

"I'm not worried about you, I'm not worried about you and I'm NOT worried about you!"

Quick Stats

DRAG RACE:
Season 3

RANKING:
7th place

SIGNATURE LOOK:
Living Pinup Realness

TYPE:
The Seasoned Queen

FAN-FAVOURITE PERFORMANCE:
"God Warrior Medley" by Various

What's the T?

A well-loved queen of the Southern California drag scene for over two decades, Delta Work (Gabriel Villarreal) was named by a fellow queen after a stint as Suzanne Sugarbaker (played by Delta Burke) in a *Designing Women* drag show. After many years as a longtime cast member of the *Dreamgirls Revue*, Delta was cast in the third season of *Drag Race* where she proved that a big girl can serve beautiful and polished runway looks, the house down! A "Heather" with a cutting sense of wit, Delta worked alongside new friends like Manila Luzon and her longtime sister Raja – the queen who first put her on stage – to give a strong performance in the competition, until falling flat in the comedy challenge. Delta Work continues to entertain across California and, in 2018, Delta's fierce work as Ru's principal wig stylist was awarded with the Primetime Emmy Award for Outstanding Hairstyling, making her the first ever Racer to snatch an Emmy award – WERK!

DELTA WORK

Derrick Barry

"It's Derrick, bitch!"

Quick Stats

DRAG RACE:
Season 8

RANKING:
5th place

SIGNATURE LOOK:
Britney Spears Realness

TYPE:
The Vegas Vixen

**FAN-FAVOURITE
PERFORMANCE:**
"Work Bitch" by Britney Spears

What's the T?

Put simply: Derrick Barry is the undisputed world's best Britney Spears drag impersonator. Initially dressing as Britney on a Halloween outing in 2003, Derrick has made an entire career out of emulating the princess of pop on The Strip in shows like Frank Marino's *Divas Las Vegas* ever since. After an unsuccessful audition for Season 7 of *Drag Race* and appearances on *America's Got Talent*, Derrick Barry was finally cast on the eighth season, where she put her best foot forward as a drag performer, instead of just a Britney impersonator. While a well known star before even making it onto the *Race*, Derrick had to work hard to prove that her drag performance, costuming, acting and comedy skills were up to scratch with on-screen rival Bob the Drag Queen. After putting up a strong fight in the *Race* and bearing her soul as a seasoned performer changing up their drag, Derrick placed fifth in the competition. Following her season, Derrick has continued to build the drag identity of "Derrick Barry" and has forged a new career as a drag princess of pop with her hot club single "Boom Boom".

DRAG TERM

Come Through

An acclamation showing congratulations of effort or performance. This phrase was famously called out in Season 7 by Violet Chachki following Katya and Kennedy Davenport's lip sync to "Roar".

DRAG TERM

Cooking

To leave makeup sitting on the face for a long
period of time so your own body heat melts the
makeup into the skin, leaving more pigmented
coverage to blend with later.

Detox

"I am the queen bee so eat it up and crown it!"

Quick Stats

DRAG RACES:
Season 5 | *All Stars* 2

RANKING:
4th place | Co-runner Up

POST DRAG RACE:
Released directorial and solo single debut "Supersonic"; featured model on *Skin Wars*; guest host on Logo's *Gay for Play* game show; sickening runway model for LA-based designer Marco Marco; appeared in 2017 film *Cherry Pop* alongside Bob the Drag Queen and Mayhem Miller; appeared on E!'s *Botched* in 2018

SIGNATURE LOOK:
Thierry Mugler Meets Jem and the Holograms Realness

TYPE:
The Style Icon

FAN-FAVOURITE PERFORMANCE:
"I Look to You" by Whitney Houston

What's the T?

A long-time star of the WeHo drag scene, Detox – the alter ego of Matthew Sanderson – channels retro 80s looks while opting for a performance style where this aesthetic is matched with a perfectly kitsch show sensibility. In her showtime staple "Nothing's Gonna Stop Us Now" by Starship, Detox marries Kim Cattrall's *Mannequin* with an outlandish 80s power suit and a frizzed weave for a perfectly camp power ballad performance. Prior to her appearance on *RuPaul's Drag Race*, Detox was a member of Californian band Tranzkuntinental alongside fellow *Drag Race* alumni Willam and Kelly Mantle.

In the lead-up to her season of *Drag Race*, Detox was easily the most recognised personality to enter that *Race* after a popular run of hit singles and music videos with her band DWV. Their 2013 single "Boy Is a Bottom" with over 20 million views, set the bar high for Detox, who only won one main challenge in her run on the show. Showing her ass literally and figuratively on the main stage, Detox channelled her camp lip sync style in all of her Lip Sync for Your Life performances, including the iconic face-off with Jinkx Monsoon to Yma Sumac's "Malambo No. 1". Her unexpected monochrome appearance at the Season 5 finale cemented Detox's status as one of the most stylish and fierce queens ever to compete in the *Race*.

After touring internationally as a solo performer after the breakup of DWV and slaying the Marco Marco runway during Los Angeles Fashion Week year after year, Detox returned to compete in the second season of *All Stars*, executing her unique sense of style and drag to place as a runner up with Katya.

DiDa Ritz

"Category is: Cheesecake!"

Quick Stats

DRAG RACE:
Season 4

RANKING:
6th place

SIGNATURE LOOK:
Wendy Williams Knowles Realness

TYPE:
"The Legs of Halsted"

**FAN-FAVOURITE
PERFORMANCE:**
"Ego" by Beyoncé

What's the T?

Having been doing drag for about four years before her appearance on the fourth season of *RuPaul's Drag Race*, DiDa Ritz (Xavier Hairston) worked the stages of Chicago, inspired by drag mother Lady Tajma Hall. Always buoyant and bubbly in the werkroom and on stage, DiDa won over audiences in the *Race* with her now iconic lip sync against The Princess, of Natalie Cole's "This Will Be (An Everlasting Love)" in front of Natalie herself (she didn't want Natalie "leaving saying that drag queen did a horrible job on my song"). Coasting through the competition safely through to sixth place, DiDa continues to entertain audiences, headlining the wildly acclaimed nationally touring the *Black Girl Magic* show alongside *Drag Race* sisters The Vixen, Monique Heart and Shea Couleé, among others.

DIDA
RITZ

Dusty
Ray
Bottom

"Neva lavd yah!"

Quick Stats

DRAG RACE:
Season 10

RANKING:
11th place

SIGNATURE LOOK:
Dots for Days Realness

TYPE:
The Punk Rock Queen

**FAN-FAVOURITE
PERFORMANCE:**
"That's Not My Name" by
The Ting Tings

What's the T?

Hailing from Louisville, Kentucky, Dusty Ray Bottoms (Dustin Rayburn) found a home in New York City chasing dreams of a career in acting after a very strict religious upbringing. The drag sister of Season 9's Alexis Michelle, Dusty embraced her musical theatre training and mashed it with a punk rock ethos to create the drag persona that was hailed by *NEXT Magazine* as "the kind of performer who just might have what it takes to rival major drag talents like RuPaul and Bianca Del Rio". A local legend, Dusty counted her own international M.A.C. Cosmetics ad campaign as a key stepping stone towards the global stage of *RuPaul's Drag Race*, where she competed in the 10th season. Though her wickedly iconic dot makeup and rocker aesthetic were polished in their own right, Dusty was sent home by Monét X Change following a poor performance in "The Last Ball on Earth" costume challenge. Following her appearance on Season 10, Dusty has focused on building her musical career, releasing killer pop rock single "Neva Lavd Yah!" in 2018 and performing on the War on the Catwalk tour of the United States.

Eureka O'Hara

"Proportionizing!"

Quick Stats

DRAG RACES:
Season 9 | Season 10

RANKING:
11th place | Co-Runner Up

SIGNATURE LOOK:
Pageant Perfection Realness

TYPE:
The High-energy Plus-size Diva

**FAN-FAVOURITE
PERFORMANCE:**
"It's My Time/Booty" by Martha Wash/
Jennifer Lopez

What's the T?

A young yet seasoned Tennessee queen of the pageant scene, Eureka O'Hara (David Huggard) has built a drag career that pushes the boundaries of what a plus-sized queen is expected to do. A high-energy dancing diva and Miss East Coast USofA at Large 2013, Eureka appeared on our screens in the ninth season of the *Race* pitted against fellow pageant competitor Trinity The Tuck, priming audiences for what could be a pageant rivalry to match that of Alyssa Edwards and Coco Montrese. Though performing strongly in the Lady Gaga and "Draggily Ever After" challenges, it was a knee injury caused by the cheerleading challenge that slowed down Eureka's streak and prompted RuPaul to ask her to leave the competition to rest, refocus and return in the 10th season of the competition.

With one season's worth of experience behind her, Eureka came into Season 10, loud, proud and with guns blazing, winning both "The Bossy Rossy Show" and "Drag Con Panel Extravaganza" challenges. With an elevated wardrobe and steely eyes on the crown, Eureka powered through to the final three-way lip sync against Aquaria and Kameron Michaels, where she won the love of fans across the world, finishing as a co-runner up. Following her time on the *Race*, the Elephant Queen has toured internationally on the Werq The World tour, has appeared in her own web series *P.H.A.T.*, and has even released her own single and music video for "The Big Girl".

Farrah Moan

"Farrah Moan: One look and your mind is blown!"

Quick Stats

DRAG RACES:
Season 9 | *All Stars* 4

RANKING:
8th place | 9th place

SIGNATURE LOOK:
Highlighted-for-the-back-row Realness

TYPE:
The Retro Glam Showgirl

FAN-FAVOURITE PERFORMANCE:
"I Want to Be Loved By You" by Sinead O'Connor

What's the T?

A young showgirl with an expensive taste for feathers and rhinestones, Farrah Moan's drag is not only inspired by the glitz and glamour of old Hollywood, but fetish fashion. A fan-favourite from the outset, Farrah (Cameron Clayton) competed in Season 9 of *Drag Race* not only blinding audiences with her highlighter but her beauty, bringing to the runway shimmering and glowing looks including an impeccable replica of Madonna's Super Bowl XLVI costume. While Farrah wasn't able to take home the crown in Season 9, the Texas-born showgirl Ru-turned to the competition in *All Stars* 4, keen on making good on her Instagram fame and forays into the world of burlesque. A literal stumble in the variety show – albeit in one of the fiercest rhinestoned costumes to ever grace the runway – marked the beginning of the end for Farrah's *All Stars* run, which lasted only three episodes. Despite not winning either *Race*, Farrah Moan continues to wow fans across the globe with sickening Instagram content and makeup tutorials – her *Cosmopolitan* transformation video has racked up over 26 million views already on Facebook. Now that's something not to moan at!

Gia Gunn

"Absolutely!"

Quick Stats

DRAG RACES:
Season 6 | *All Stars* 4

RANKING:
10th place | 8th place

SIGNATURE LOOK:
Banjee Glam Geisha Realness

TYPE:
The Fresh Tilapia Queen

FAN-FAVOURITE PERFORMANCE:
"Kabuki/Ru Girl Mix" by Various

What's the T?

Landing fresh off the boat direct from a little trip in Asia, like fresh tilapia, Chicago's Gia Gunn (Gia Ichikawa) has been entertaining audiences in drag since she was seven years old, which is when she started performing in traditional Japanese kabuki theatre as an onnagata (a male actor who plays a woman's role). While "feeling her oats" in the sixth season of *Drag Race*, Gia lit up screens with her countless catchphrases and turned out fabulous looks on the main stage before fatefully meeting her match in a lip sync battle against her new sister Laganja Estranja. Following her appearance on the *Race*, Gia had gone from strength to strength professionally, releasing singles with Alaska ("Stun" in 2017 and "La China Más Latina" in 2018) and finishing runner up in the second season of Chilean drag competition program *The Switch Drag Race* before appearing on *All Stars* 4 as her authentic and absolutely feisty and fierce transgender self. While delivering a stellar traditional kabuki performance for the All Stars Variety Show (she was robbed!), sickening runways and an adrenalin-raising lip sync performance against Naomi Smalls, it was Gia's behind-the-scenes shade during the season that got her competitors and some fans calling her the "villain of the season". All drama aside, Gia Gunn delivers equal doses of good shade, good show and good TV – a true *Drag Race* All Star!

Ginger Minj

"I'm a crossdresser for Christ. I'll have you down on your knees..."

Quick Stats

DRAG RACES:
Season 7 | *All Stars* 2

RANKING:
Co-runner Up | 8th place

POST DRAG RACE:
Toured her solo shows *Crossdresser for Christ* in 2015 and *Truly Divine* tributing the late great drag icon Divine in 2018; released debut album *Sweet T* in 2016; starred in Netflix comedy *Dumplin'*

SIGNATURE LOOK:
Glamour Toad Realness

TYPE:
The Comedy Queen of the South

FAN-FAVOURITE PERFORMANCE:
"The Edge of Glory" by Lady Gaga

What's the T?

Hailing from Orlando, Joshua Allan Eads has performed in the pageant circuit as Ginger Minj across the South for the best part of the 2010s, earning her the titles of Miss Gay United States 2013 and Miss National Comedy Queen 2012. Inspired by Ginger, her favourite character on the 60s TV show *Gilligan's Island*, Minj had performed in the theatre since the age of four. A young queen in love with the classic funny ladies of yesteryear, she hosted *Broadway Brunch* in 2013 at Hamburger Mary's in Orlando – a full-scale musical production with a cast of 15, with drag sister The Minx.

Following performances in the Orlando theatre scene in shows including *Chicago*, *Gypsy* and *The Wiz*, Ginger Minj competed in the seventh season of *Drag Race*. A plus-size queen and fan-favourite, Ginger harnessed all her theatrical gusto to win the musical theatre challenge and give a memorable tribute to John Waters' *Pink Flamingos* in the parody "Eggs". Her strong performance in the competition pushed her to the final three where she came in as co-runner up with Pearl, leading to her casting on the second season of *All Stars*. Although she didn't last long in the *All Star* race, she gave a fabulous vocal performance in the talent show extravaganza.

Following in the footsteps of *Drag Race* alumni Jinkx Monsoon, Ginger Minj has taken her powerful vocal ability, showgirl prowess and love for the classic era of cinema and created *Crossdresser for Christ* – a confessional musical chronicling her own drag evolution and life story.

Drag mother

A drag mother is a person who indoctrinates a young queen into the world of drag, guiding creative decisions and supporting the younger queen's forays into the art form. Shangela and Laganja Estranja both identify Alyssa Edwards as their drag mother; a queen who not only put them into drag in the early stages of their career but has been a mentor throughout.

Dusted

The opposite of "busted", "dusted" describes a queen who appears flawless and polished in their drag transformation. Chad Michaels is often referred to as "Mother Dust", suggesting Chad is not only professional and polished, but a drag queen to look up to for inspiration.

Honey Mahogany

"People get down on San Francisco... but there is so much beauty there – have you seen Honey Mahogany?"

Quick Stats

DRAG RACE:
Season 5

RANKING:
10th/11th place

SIGNATURE LOOK:
Bed Bath & Beyond Realness

TYPE:
San Fran Glamour Queen

FAN-FAVOURITE PERFORMANCE:
"It's Honey" by Honey Mahogany

What's the T?

A creative yet socially conscious queen and the first ever from San Francisco to be cast on *Drag Race*, Honey Mahogany (Alpha Mulugeta) began her drag career while studying, co-founding Berkeley University's *Next Top Drag Performer* on-campus contest. Influenced by 60s and 70s glamour, Honey's appearance on the fifth season of the *Race* was short-lived – cancelled by the collection of kaftans that she wore on the main stage runway. While not getting a chance to showcase her vocal talents on the show, Honey Mahogany continued to gag her fans with dance single "It's Honey" and went on to release her own EP in 2014 titled *Honey Love*.

India
Ferrah

"Get her off of me!"

Quick Stats

DRAG RACE:
Season 3

RANKING:
10th place

SIGNATURE LOOK:
Breastplate Babe Realness

TYPE:
High-glam Dancing Queen

**FAN–FAVOURITE
PERFORMANCE:**
"Tens Medley" by Jennifer Lopez
& Various

What's the T?

An All American Goddess pageant winner before her 21st birthday in 2008, Virginia's India Ferrah (Shane Richardson) had learned the ropes of entertaining and snatching pageant crowns long before other queens could legally drink! After unsuccessfully auditioning for the first two seasons of *Drag Race*, India (along with her iconic $600 breastplate) was cast in the third season where she brought a sense of old-school glamour and new-school dance and performance style to the runway. A fumble in the "QNN News" reporter challenge saw India eliminated early in the contest. However, inspired by criticism of her time on the show, India Ferrah moved to Las Vegas in 2012, where she has elevated her drag to true showgirl status and is now considered one of the top performers on The Strip.

Ivy Winters

"Ivyyyyyyyyyyyyyy
Winterrrrrrrrrrrrs!"

Quick Stats

DRAG RACE:
Season 5

RANKING:
7th place (Miss Congeniality)

SIGNATURE LOOK:
High Concept Couture Realness

TYPE:
The Creative Circus Queen

**FAN-FAVOURITE
PERFORMANCE:**
"Titanium" by David Guetta ft. Sia

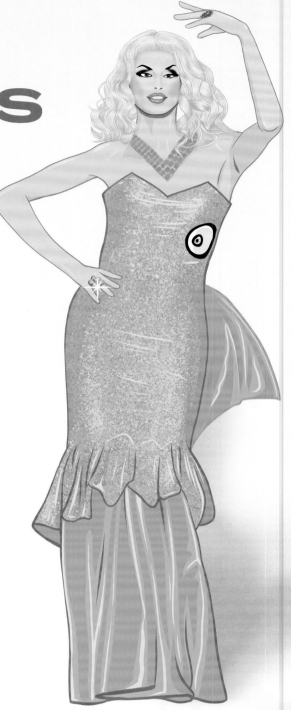

What's the T?

An actor, singer, former clown, and costumier in New York City dressing queens including Lady Bunny and Manila Luzon, Ivy Winters (Dustin Winters) is easily one of the strongest contestants to have ever competed in the *Race*. Demonstrating her style and circus artistry, Ivy stomped the runway in intricate costumes ranging from Victor/Victoria recreations to a newspaper cocktail dress to a larger-than-life butterfly on stilts! One of the nicest queens on *Drag Race*, Ivy snatched the title of Miss Congeniality, toured the world with the Battle of the Seasons tour in 2016 and even clay-animated the music video for her Christmas single "Elfy Winters Night".

IVY
WINTERS

Jade Jolie

"Serving up fish – tuna on a platter."

Quick Stats

DRAG RACE:
Season 5

RANKING:
8th place

SIGNATURE LOOK:
Lisa Frank Realness

TYPE:
The Kaleidoscopic Queen

FAN-FAVOURITE PERFORMANCE:
"Harley Quinn Medley" by Various

What's the T?

Just like her namesake Angelina, Jade Jolie (Josh Green) serves fabulous mug, a polished aesthetic and larger-than-life looks for the children! Appropriately cast in what Alaska admits was the "Season of the Fish" (Season 5), Jade Jolie demonstrated not only sweet and colourful runway presentations but helped coin one of the most iconic catchphrases after a heated fight over human-hair wigs with Alyssa Edwards: "Girl – you had rolls all over the place in the back...". Feel free to clap back to that read! A self-proclaimed "gaymer" and fan of cosplay, Jade continues to harness pop culture to create shows and killer looks that are not only loved by club-goers across the United States but also by her 120k+ followers on Instagram.

JADE
JOLIE

Jade Soto-mayor

"Jade is definitely my alter-ego... she has more balls than I do!"

Quick Stats

DRAG RACE:
Season 1

RANKING:
6th place

SIGNATURE LOOK:
J-To-Tha-L-O Realness

TYPE:
Latina Queen of Dance

FAN–FAVOURITE PERFORMANCE:
"I Need Your Love "by Calvin Harris ft. Ellie Goulding

What's the T?

Having worked for years as a professional dancer and choreographer in Chicago, David Sotomayor made his debut as Jade in 2003, inspired by the Latin queens of pop, particularly Jennifer Lopez. Utilising her skills as a dancer and her fabulous Latin flair, Jade gave a solid performance in the very first season of *Drag Race*, showcasing her dance abilities in the girl group challenge and her soft side in the "M.A.C. Viva-Glam" challenge.

Jade has built on her status as one of the original Racers, performing across the States, on the Al and Chuck Drag Stars at Sea cruises and also returned to our screens performing "Born Naked" alongside Monique Heart in the Season 10 finale, shimmering in a fierce gold warrior ensemble celebrating 10 years of the program's success.

JADE MAYOR

Jaidynn Diore Fierce

"No ma'am, no ham, no pam, no cauliflower, no corn bread, no green beans!"

Quick Stats

DRAG RACE:
Season 7

RANKING:
8th place

SIGNATURE LOOK:
Outerspace City Babe Realness

TYPE:
Curvy Queen of Dance

FAN-FAVOURITE PERFORMANCE:
"Single Ladies" by Beyoncé

What's the T?

Starting her drag career at the age of 22, Jaidynn Diore Fierce (Christopher Williams) rocked the Nashville drag scene before bringing her larger-than-life vibrancy and edgy performance style to the main stage of *RuPaul's Drag Race* in Season 7. A pageant queen with one hell of a mug, Jaidynn brought the energy each week in the competition and, while having to lip sync for her life three times, she showed audiences exactly why a big girl can hold it with the rest of them! Following her time on the *Race* Jaidynn has focused on her collaborations with WOWPresents and her own channel on YouTube, creating *Drag Race* after-show reviews and makeup tutorials.

Jasmine Masters

"No tea, no shade, no pink lemonade!"

Quick Stats

DRAG RACES:
Season 7 | *All Stars* 4

RANKING:
12th place | 10th place

SIGNATURE LOOK:
Patti LaBelle Pageant Realness

TYPE:
The Old School Diva

**FAN-FAVOURITE
PERFORMANCE:**
"NeNe Leakes Mix" by Various

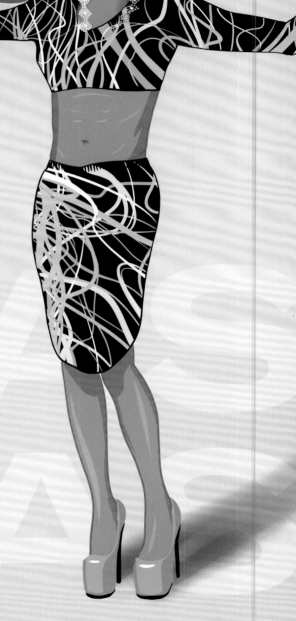

What's the T?

An old-school queen with so much new-school relevance and a meme-able sense of humour like no other, California's Jasmine Masters (Martell Robinson) has spent over 20 years honing her skills as a masterful queen of comedy and impersonation; her Patti LaBelle is EVERYTHING! Having already won over YouTube audiences with her "I'm Jasmine Masters and I have something to say…" series, RuPaul decided, as Jasmine was one of her own favourite performers, that it was time for her to compete in the *Race*. Though she floundered in the competition, her catchphrases and impeccable sense of humour won over audiences, even if she was dubbed "the poster child of discontent". Jasmine's status as "the meme queen" led to her casting on both the *Holi-Slay Spectacular* and the fourth season of *All Stars*; albeit not for long as she was first to be booted after a cringe-tastic comedy routine. Despite her short lived appearances on the *Race*, Jasmine has continued to work and "get her jush" (check out her Instagram for explanations on this one!) in the Southern California drag circuit, blessed audiences with her own WOW Presents web series *Jasmine Masters' Class* and has found new fans in her viral videos after Justin Bieber and other celebrities re-circulated snippets of her iconic rants.

DRAG TERM

Fishy

A term to describe a queen's ability to appear
exceptionally feminine when in drag, irrespective of
how little or much makeup is used to create the gender
illusion. The term refers to the colloquial likening
of the scent of a woman's genitals to that of fish.
While considered its own form of drag presentation,
queens described as "fishy" on *RuPaul's Drag Race*
are often asked by the judges to not "rest on pretty"
or rely on their body to succeed in the competition.
See: Courtney Act, Farrah Moan, Kenya Michaels,
Rebecca Glasscock, Carmen Carrera.

DRAG TERM

Flazéda

A mishmash of "blasé" and "laissez-faire", the
term "flazéda" was coined by Pearl in Season 7
to convey an air of nonchalance and being relaxed,
yet actually being in total control.

Jaymes Mansfield

"These are my summer diamonds – some are diamonds, some are not!"

Quick Stats

DRAG RACE:
Season 9

RANKING:
14th place

SIGNATURE LOOK:
Teddy Bear Couture Realness

TYPE:
The Hilarious Herstorian

**FAN-FAVOURITE
PERFORMANCE:**
"The Homecoming Queen's
Got a Gun" by Julie Brown

What's the T?

Inspired by characters like Elvira and Pee Wee Herman, Milwaukee's Jaymes Mansfield (James Wirth) fleshed out her larger-than-life drag persona while building her YouTube channel over the last two years, before being cast as one of the bubbly and camp queens of Season 9 of *Drag Race*.

Unfortunately Jaymes didn't get much of a chance to show off her comedic talents nor her wacky wardrobe, which has won over her social media fans, as she was eliminated first from the contest. Refusing to let the elimination put a hole in her sail, Jaymes has continued to produce content for her channel, building on an already impressive pre-*Race* fanbase with her costume and makeup tutorial videos and her incredibly well researched and presented *Drag HerStory* series.

Jessica Wild

"I love that drink!"

Quick Stats

DRAG RACE:
Season 2

RANKING:
6th place

SIGNATURE LOOK:
Puerto Rican Pop Star Realness

TYPE:
The Escandalo Sweetheart

**FAN-FAVOURITE
PERFORMANCE:**
"Absolutely" by Jessica Wild

What's the T?

Born and raised in San Juan, Puerto Rico, Jessica Wild (José David Sierra) harnessed her skills as a dance choreographer and makeup artist to create a high-energy drag persona that saw her move to Miami to pursue a career as a showgirl. Chosen by the viewers online in a casting competition, Jessica appeared in the second season of *RuPaul's Drag Race*, serving not only wondrously wild costumes and hair, but a strong sense of confidence and humility. Performing strongly throughout her season, winning the "Rocker Chicks" live singing challenge, Jessica was closely beaten by the sensual performance of Tatianna in a Lip Sync for Your Life battle. Following her appearance on the *Race*, Jessica Wild has continued to perform across the US, released the dance singles "You Like It Wild" and "Absolutely" and even impersonated pop star Selena on Bravo's *Watch What Happens Live*.

Jiggly Caliente

"I went from a baked potato to a sweet potato!"

Quick Stats

DRAG RACE:
Season 4

RANKING:
8th place

SIGNATURE LOOK:
Straight off the Subway Realness

TYPE:
The NYC Asian Plus Size Barbie

FAN-FAVOURITE
PERFORMANCE:
"I Don't Give a F***" by Jiggly Caliente

What's the T?

With a name inspired by a Pokémon, New York's Jiggly Caliente (Bianca Castro) is a queen who serves ghetto fabulous like no other and can boast the title of winning her first drag contest on her first night of drag as Jiggly! As sweet as candy and as loud as a firecracker, Jiggly's appearance on the fourth season of *Drag Race* was met with both laughter at her jokes (and her baked potato couture runway in the first episode) and admiration for her fierceness in a lip sync battle. While her runways didn't always win over the judges, Jiggly kept audiences gagging for her onscreen puffs with her fellow queens, never letting the fans down on seeing the fiery Filipina hold it down with the shadiest of queens in the Untucked lounge. Since competing on the *Race*, Jiggly has toured the world, released a killer rap debut record, "T.H.O.T. Process", and come out as transgender, inspiring her fans far and wide to live their truth.

Jinkx Monsoon

"I'm Seattle's youngest MILF."

Quick Stats

DRAG RACE:
Season 5

RANKING:
Winner

POST DRAG RACE:
Toured off-Broadway musical comedy
The Vaudevillians internationally;
released albums *The Inevitable Album*
(2014), *ReAnimated* (2015), *The Ginger
Snapped* (2018); starred as the subject
of documentary film and web series
Drag Becomes Him (2015)

SIGNATURE LOOK:
Jewish MILF Realness

TYPE:
The Broadway Queen

**FAN-FAVOURITE
PERFORMANCE:**
"Malambo No. 1" by Yma Sumac

What's the T?

Performing in drag for the first time at 15, Jerick Hoffer began his onstage career with performances at underage nightclub Escape and dance club The Streets in his hometown of Portland, Oregon. Following a move to Seattle, Jinkx Monsoon emerged in a series of *Funny or Die* webisodes called *Monsoon Season*. A queen of all media and stage platforms, Jinkx continued her work in musical theatre with appearances in *Spring Awakening* and *Rent* as well as taking the title role in *Hedwig and the Angry Inch* in 2013. Prior to her appearance on *Drag Race* Jinkx became the subject of YouTube docu-series *Drag Becomes Him*, exploring her life as Jerick and as Jinkx. This web series led to a film adaptation in 2015.

Inspired by the high-concept characterisation of Season 4 winner Sharon Needles, Monsoon auditioned and landed a position on the fifth season of *Drag Race*. A dark horse throughout, Jinkx was constantly pressured by fellow competitors and judges on the merits of her costuming and makeup skills. However, she persevered to prove that she didn't need to be the fishiest, most glamorous queen – she was a superstar in her own right. Not only winning the main challenges for the "Snatch Game" (in her iconic performance of Little Edie Beale) and "Drama Queens", Jinkx went on to take the crown over fan-favourite Alaska and pageant superstar Roxxxy Andrews.

Following her win, Jinkx worked on bringing the show *The Vaudevillians* to a wider audience. Through major performances of the show off-Broadway and as part of the Sydney Mardi Gras, Jinkx demonstrated that she was a different kind of winner from her predecessors – she was the drag Andrew Lloyd Webber!

Joslyn Fox

"Keep it foxy – wonk wonk!"

Quick Stats

DRAG RACE:
Season 6

RANKING:
6th place

SIGNATURE LOOK:
Glamourpuss Realness

TYPE:
The Stone Cold Fox

FAN-FAVOURITE PERFORMANCE:
"Medley" by Janet Jackson

What's the T?

As a musical theatre kid only 20 years old, Patrick Joslyn discovered that his love of pop stars, hair and makeup artistry, and music editing could be forged into an exciting career as Joslyn Fox – the stone cold fox of Massachusetts. Having auditioned four times for *Drag Race*, Joslyn made her way onto Season 6 where she was immediately poised to compete with her personal drag idol Courtney Act. The self-proclaimed "black horse", Joslyn worked her way through the competition with a sense of fun and positivity, which may not have won her the title of Miss Congeniality, but won the hearts of viewers who were by her side as she gave her surprise wedding vows at the live Season 6 reunion – with Mama Ru presiding over the ceremony of course! Joslyn Fox has continued to enjoy success as a touring Racer and starred in Bianca Del Rio's debut film *Hurricane Bianca*.

Jujubee

"I like long walks on the beach, big dicks and fried chicken."

Quick Stats

DRAG RACES:
Season 2 | *All Stars* 1

RANKINGS:
3rd place | 3rd/4th place

POST DRAG RACE:
Star of *RuPaul's Drag Race* spin-offs *Drag U* and *Drag My Dinner Party* with Raven and Manila Luzon; guest stars on WOWPresents viral videos including *Fashion Photo RuView* with Raven and *Bestie$ for Ca$h*

SIGNATURE LOOK:
Memoirs of a Gay-sha Realness

TYPE:
The First Lady of Lip Sync

FAN–FAVOURITE PERFORMANCE:
"Dancing on My Own" (with Raven during *All Stars* 1) by Robyn

What's the T?

Born from the drag scene of Boston, Massachusetts, Jujubee – the creation of Airline Inthyrath – was the creative fusion of her many years of studying theatre at the University of Massachusetts and her cultural upbringing as a Laotian American. Jujubee's aesthetic is often giving a cheeky nod to her Asian heritage while fusing traditional drag aesthetic and a slick street style.

A star from the second season of *Drag Race*, Jujubee won the hearts of the public despite never winning a main challenge. Her quick wit, warm disposition and cut-throat reading skills – "Miss Tyra, was your barbecue cancelled? Your grill is fucked up!" – pushed the Laotian goddess through to the top three of the competition. Described as the first lady of lip sync, Jujubee is one of the most iconic performers in the herstory of *RuPaul's Drag Race* and despite having found herself five times in the bottom two, never lost a single lip sync. Her performances to "Black Velvet" by Alannah Myles and Robyn's "Dancing on My Own" (with Raven on *All Stars*) remain undisputed demonstrations of incomparable drag performance.

Her additional appearances as a mainstay professor on the spin-offs *Drag U* and *Drag My Dinner Party* with Manila Luzon and Raven have helped boost Jujubee's social media reach, earning her a legion of fans on Facebook and Instagram giving her the status of one of the most followed queens from the earlier *Drag Race* seasons.

Kalorie Karbdashian-Williams

"Hope you're ready for your all-Karb, high-Kalorie diet!"

Quick Stats

DRAG RACE:
Season 10

RANKING:
13th place

SIGNATURE LOOK:
Rhinestone Bodysuit Eleganza

TYPE:
The Wicked Kardashian Step-sister

FAN-FAVOURITE PERFORMANCE:
"Hero Medley" by Various

What's the T?

New Mexico's Kalorie Karbdashian-Williams (Daniel Hernandez) started her drag career in 2013, serving up equal parts Kardashian glamour and big-girl ferocity to snatch pageant wins including Miss Duke City 2016. A fan of *Drag Race* and thick and juicy queens like Roxxxy Andrews, Kalorie entered the Season 10 werkroom determined to prove her performing talents but found herself in the bottom two straight off the bat for a style misstep in the first challenge. Showing that there was more to her than crunchy cash couture, Kalorie served up all the Aguilera vibes needed to eliminate her competition – Vanessa Vanjie Mateo – in a show-stopping performance of "Ain't No Other Man". Despite making it to the second week, Kalorie stumbled in the "PharmaRusical" challenge, fading into the pack of queens and eventually eliminated after her cute and curvy rhinestoned runway presentation.

Since *Drag Race*, Kalorie has spoken out against fan bullying, which she encountered after sending Miss Vanjie home in the first week, and has toured the United States serving up boundless Latina glamour – her "Día de los Muertos" realness at DragCon 2018 in particular slayed!

DRAG TERM

For the gods

A way to describe something as being done to
perfection or to describe something as fabulous.
For example: "Mariah's face is beat for the gods!".

DRAG TERM

Gag

To react intensely, as a result of shock. To "gag"
on a drag queen's "eleganza" is to be absolutely
floored by the fabulous artistry and aesthetic
that said queen is presenting. The term can also
be used as an exclamation of satisfaction:
"Gag!" – Manila Luzon.

Kameron Michaels

"Well I auditioned for Pit Crew, but this is gonna be way more fun!"

Quick Stats

DRAG RACE:
Season 10

RANKING:
Co-runner Up

SIGNATURE LOOK:
Elven Princess Realness

TYPE:
The Bodybuilder Barbie

FAN-FAVOURITE PERFORMANCE:
"No Excuses" by Meghan Trainor

What's the T?

A hairstylist by day, lip sync assassin by night, Kameron Michaels (Dane Young) from Nashville, Tennessee – the home of some seriously good drag! – got her start at the age of 18 while working as a go-go boy inspired by video games and fantasy characters. Facing criticism from her peers for her muscles conflicting with the feminine aesthetic that comes with her drag, Kameron found herself taking breaks from drag before realising that she could embrace the masculine and feminine to create the persona that fans came to adore on Season 10 of *Drag Race*. While countless killer looks and performances, including a Maleficent-inspired feather runway, and her 1960s Cher live impersonation, cemented her position in the competition, Kameron's quiet disposition placed her lower in some of the comedic challenges. Having lip synced for her life a total of six times (!) consecutively in the second half of Season 10, Kameron proved that her performance chops outweigh any shyness and ultimately landed her in the position of co-runner up alongside Tennessee sister Eureka.

Since *Drag Race* Kameron has toured the world as part of the 10s Across the Board and Werq The World tours and even hit #12 on the Billboard Dance/Electronic Songs Chart for the single "American", which she featured on, alongside RuPaul, Aquaria, Asia O'Hara and Eureka.

Kandy Ho

"I hope you girls have got a sweet tooth 'cause Kandy's in the motherfucking house!"

Quick Stats

DRAG RACE:
Season 7

RANKING:
10th place

SIGNATURE LOOK:
Glamour Ho Realness

TYPE:
The All-powerful Performer

FAN-FAVOURITE PERFORMANCE:
"Robotika" by Various

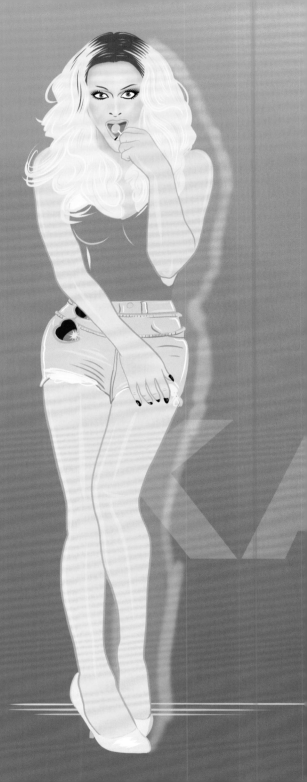

What's the T?

Hailing from the YouTube-famous *Doll House* – a Puerto Rican drag troupe of glamazons with out-of-this-world performance skills – is Kandy Ho (Frank Diaz), a pageant queen who made it onto the seventh season of *Drag Race*. Championed by her viral performances online, fans were eager to see Kandy take charge on the main stage of *Drag Race* only to be met with lacklustre performances in the acting challenge-heavy season. A gorgeous queen with a slick sense of choreography and show production, Kandy has continued to perform across the United States and Puerto Rico and competed alongside Gia Gunn in the second season of Chilean television program *The Switch Drag Race.*

ANDY HO

Mrs. Kasha Davis

"There's always time for a cocktail!"

Quick Stats

DRAG RACE:
Season 7

RANKING:
11th place

SIGNATURE LOOK:
Real Housewife of Rochester Realness

TYPE:
The Mother Hen

FAN-FAVOURITE PERFORMANCE:
"Cocktail" by Mrs. Kasha Davis

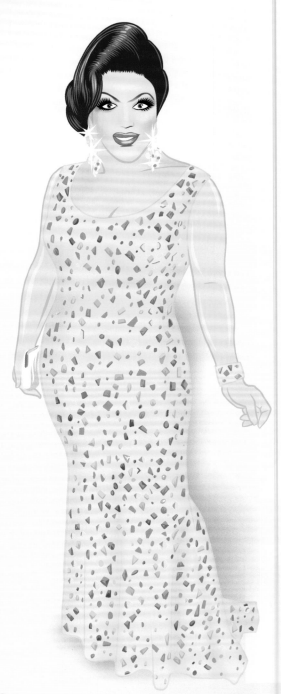

What's the T?

Inspired by the character of Miss Richfield 1981 and under the guidance of drag mother Naomi Kane, Mrs. Kasha Davis (Ed Popil) has become one of Rochester, New York's shining drag starlets alongside sisters Pandora Boxx and Darienne Lake. A laugh-out-loud kinda gal with a slick singing ability and a penchant for boxed wine, Kasha auditioned for all six previous seasons of *Drag Race* before finally being cast in the seventh, where she won audiences over with her effervescent character and high-glamour housewife aesthetic. One of the "bitter old lady brigade", Kasha nailed the "Glamazonian Airways" challenge, bringing to audiences a strong sense of old-school camp and kitsch to a season full of new-school Instagram-famous queens. While her exit was untimely and the result of a stumble hosting the "DESPY Awards", her return in the "Conjoined Queens" challenge alongside DESPY co-host Katya was a Banger Sisters dream come true – with the two's conjoined crotch-couture reminding audiences the value of good ole-fashioned crass drag. Since her time on *Drag Race*, Mrs. Kasha Davis has continued to evoke belly laughs online with web series *Life with the Davises* (co-starring Mr. Davis!) and her first one-woman world-touring cabaret show *There's Always Time for a Cocktail*.

Katya

"I'm just your average run-of-the-mill Russian bisexual transvestite hooker."

Quick Stats

DRAG RACES:
Season 7 | *All Stars* 2

RANKING:
5th place (Miss Congeniality) |
Co-runner Up

POST DRAG RACE:
Performs "12 Days of Christmas" on the *Christmas Queens* album (2015); featured on RuPaul's single "Read U Wrote U" (2016); star of *The Trixie & Katya Show* on Viceland; starred in *Hurricane Bianca 2: From Russia with Hate* (2018)

SIGNATURE LOOK:
Russian Bombshell Realness

TYPE:
The Cold War Comedy Sweetheart

FAN-FAVOURITE PERFORMANCE:
"All That Jazz" (In Russian) from *Chicago (Original Soundtrack)*

What's the T?

Katya Zamolodchikova – everyone's favourite Russian doll – was born from the mind of Boston's Brian McCook. Inspired by the comedy genius of Amy Sedaris, Tracey Ullman and Maria Bamford, and Russian songstress Alla Pugacheva, Katya's humour is the perfect blend of random hilarity and Soviet sass. A high concept character like Tammie Brown or Sharon Needles, Katya sees herself as a "retired kindergarten teacher that becomes a street-walking psychic crime fighter who's also battling depression and schizophrenia".

One of the front runners from the get go, Katya served not only glamour but camp in her performances throughout *Drag Race*. An early Lip Sync for Your Life performance to Olivia Newton-John's "Twist of Fate" in a perfectly floral patterned air hostess outfit was enough fire under Katya to inspire very strong performances in the John Waters inspired "Divine Inspiration", "Ru Hollywood Stories" and "Prancing Queens" challenges. Although coming in fifth place, Katya took out the title of Miss Congeniality for Season 7.

As a fan-favourite of her season, Katya found new fame online with fellow Racer Trixie Mattel in their World of Wonder produced series *UNHhhh* – a brilliantly random segment where the two talk about whatever they want, because it's their show and not yours! – which morphed into the Viceland television series *The Trixie & Katya Show*. Katya returned stronger than ever in the second *All Stars* season, winning three main challenges, placing as a runner up alongside Detox, reminding audiences that she's "the only high class Russian whore" to take the drag world (and your dad) by storm.

Following her time on *Drag Race* and *All Stars*, Katya has toured extensively and as a result had to take time off in 2018 to focus on her mental health, all the while dissecting these positive and negative life experiences in her very own podcast *Whimsically Volatile*.

Kelly Mantle

"Don't they know who I think I am?"

Quick Stats

DRAG RACE:
Season 6

RANKING:
13th/14th place

SIGNATURE LOOK:
Drag Rocker Realness

TYPE:
The Television Queen

FAN-FAVOURITE PERFORMANCE:
"My Neck, My Back (Lick It)" by Kelly Mantle

What's the T?

Anyone who's watched American television in the last 15 years or so will have caught a glimpse of drag actress extraordinaire Kelly Mantle. Appearing on shows like *Nip/Tuck* (alongside *Drag Race* sister Willam), *LAPD Blue*, *The New Normal* and *Curb Your Enthusiasm*, Kelly Mantle has built a career as a go-to queen when drag performers are cast on screen, but she has also built a solid career as a live performer with band Tranzkuntinental. Possibly one of the strongest "first-out" of the *Race*, Season 6 was unfortunately a short ride for Mantle, whose bacon-esque blouse didn't win over the judges in the first week costuming challenge. Following the *Race*, Kelly has continued to pursue her music career with single "Keyboard Courage" as well as her acting career with a performance in 2014's *Confessions of a Womanizer*, which made headlines as the film's producers sought to nominate Mantle for both supporting actor and actress considerations at the Academy Awards for her performance being a gender-fluid person.

Kennedy Davenport

"I didn't die, bitch,
I crystallized and now I'm
a glamazon bitch, ready
for the runway."

Quick Stats

DRAG RACES:
Season 7 | *All Stars* 3

RANKING:
4th place | 2nd place

SIGNATURE LOOK:
Polished Pageant Queen Realness

TYPE:
The Dancing Diva of Dallas

**FAN-FAVOURITE
PERFORMANCE:**
"Last Dance" by Donna Summer

What's the T?

Hailing from the legendary Davenport dynasty of Texas, Kennedy Davenport (Reuben Asberry Jr.) has built her drag career since the age of 16, working her way through the pageant scene of the South, under the guidance of her drag mother Kelexis, to win a swag of titles including Mid America All American Goddess 2013. A strong contender for the crown in the seventh season of *Drag Race*, Kennedy won over audiences with a killer impersonation of Little Richard in the "Snatch Game" and her high-kicking power-split lip sync to Katy Perry's "Roar" against Katya.

Entering the *All Stars* 3 werkroom as the fiercest human disco ball you've ever seen, Kennedy delivered sparkling runway presentations and slayed in her shelarious "Bitchelor" challenge performance. In an unexpected twist executed by the eliminated queens, Kennedy progressed to the top two of the competition giving a powerful and heartfelt lip sync performance of Miley Cyrus' "Wrecking Ball" against Trixie Mattel. Although she didn't enter the All Stars Hall of Fame, Kennedy Davenport continues to follow her dream of incorporating live vocals into her act and released her first dance single "Moving Up" in 2018.

Kenya Michaels

"I'm a little person, but I'm FIERCE... BITCH!"

Quick Stats

DRAG RACE:
Season 4

RANKING:
5th place (originally 9th)

SIGNATURE LOOK:
Petite Beauty Queen Realness

TYPE:
The Pint Sized Perra

FAN-FAVOURITE PERFORMANCE:
"Shakira Medley" by Shakira

What's the T?

A gorgeous and effervescent Puerto Rican queen, Kenya Michaels (Kenya Olivera) gave her first ever female impersonation act as Celia Cruz at the age of 15 as a gift to her sister for her birthday. A creative queen with a killer dance ability and a strong sense of fierce, Kenya wowed both her fellow cast and audiences in the fourth season of *RuPaul's Drag Race* with her unmatched beauty in such a little package. Although safe throughout most of the competition, Kenya was eliminated after a wacky and frankly out-of-character impersonation of Beyoncé in the "Snatch Game" only to be brought back for the makeover challenge, which she lost in a now iconic lip sync to "(You Make Me Feel Like) A Natural Woman" against Latrice Royale. Coming out as transgender following her time on the *Race*, Kenya has continued to produce and perform shows in Florida as well as release her own men's fashion line.

DRAG TERM

Geish

A term originated from Geisha – a Japanese
female entertainer – "geish" refers to a drag
queen's makeup and wardrobe. To be completely
dressed in drag can be described as "in geish".

DRAG TERM

Giving me life

To say something is "giving me life" means that something has got you wildly excited. For example "Girl, Violet Chachki's waist in that Death Becomes Her runway is giving me LIFE!".

Kim Chi

"Donut come for me!"

Quick Stats

DRAG RACE:
Season 8

RANKING:
Co-runner Up

SIGNATURE LOOK:
Pastel Fantasy Realness

TYPE:
The Kawaii Queen

**FAN-FAVOURITE
PERFORMANCE:**
"Fat, Fem & Asian" by Lucian Piane

What's the T?

Chicago's priestess of pastel with a taste for over-the-top high-concept fashion, Kim Chi (Sang-Young Shin) started playing with drag in 2012 with *Drag Race* sister Pearl, quickly perfecting her unique brand of often Asian-inspired drag. Exhibiting the sheer creativity, mastery and level of research skill that many Asian drag queens possess, Kim Chi appeared on the eighth season of *Drag Race* where she placed as runner up, claiming two costume creation challenge wins and essentially slaying the main stage runway from week to week. Winning over audiences in the *Race* has only been the start for Kim Chi, who has gone on to release several makeup lines with brand Sugar Pill, to tour South Korea, star in her own web series *M.U.G.* with Naomi Smalls, and release a line of hydrating face masks depicting her iconic makeup looks. Oh, and she is also one of the most popular queens on Instagram with more than 1.7 million followers!

CHI

Kimora Blac

"Kimora Blac is everyone's sexual preference!"

Quick Stats

DRAG RACE:
Season 9

RANKING:
13th place

SIGNATURE LOOK:
Body-ody-ody-suit Realness

TYPE:
The Boujee Barbie

FAN-FAVOURITE PERFORMANCE:
"Sex Shooter" by Cahill ft. Nikki Belle

What's the T?

A huge fan of transformation, playing with drag from the age of 15, Las Vegas vixen Kimora Blac (Von Nguyen) has built a drag persona for more than 10 years, which sells seduction and sex like no other. An Instagram star boasting more than 300,000 fans, Kimora has channelled her inner Kim K, not only in her aesthetic, but in creating a brand of drag that leaves her fans wanting to gag on more of her incredible transformations. While her time on the ninth season of *Drag Race* was short-lived, she managed to leave the competition with a connection to the drag community that she didn't feel she had prior, when she was a working showgirl on the Vegas Strip. Kimora Blac continues to wow audiences with her porn star-meets-Kardashian realness while bringing home the laughs with her very own WOWPresents web series *Wait, What?*, which she co-hosts with Mariah, Gia Gunn and Derrick Barry.

Laganja Estranja

"OKUURRRRRRR!"

Quick Stats

DRAG RACE:
Season 6

RANKING:
8th place

POST DRAG RACE:
Tours internationally with the Haus of Edwards alongside drag family Alyssa Edwards and Shangela; released singles "Legs" (2015) and "Look At Me" (2018); choreographed the Miley Cyrus performance of "Dooo It!" 2015 MTV Video Music Awards

SIGNATURE LOOK:
Mary Jane Girl Realness

TYPE:
The Sickening Stoner

FAN-FAVOURITE PERFORMANCE:
"Beyoncé Medley" (with Barbie's Addiction) by Beyoncé

What's the T?

A member of the legendary Haus of Edwards, Laganja Estranja (Jay Jackson) emerged from years working as a choreographer with Alyssa Edwards' Beyond Belief Dance Company in Dallas. Following a move to study in California, Laganja honed her drag talents alongside newcomer Adore Delano and went on to win a drag contest at Micky's in West Hollywood and subsequently a monthly guest spot alongside *Drag Race* alumni at the famed Showgirls drag night. A sickening dancer and performer, Laganja quickly took the LA drag scene by storm with her dancing troupe Barbie's Addiction.

Although still a newcomer to drag, Laganja was cast in the sixth season of *RuPaul's Drag Race* following in the footsteps of drag mother Alyssa Edwards and sister Shangela. While a fan-favourite from the outset, Laganja's performance through the season was green (pun intended) and lacked the experience of her competitors. Despite receiving a lot of tough love from the judges and Bianca Del Rio, Laganja went on to win one major challenge and finished eighth after two strong lip syncs against Gia Gunn and Joslyn Fox.

Determined to prove her star quality and exceptional dance skills, Laganja has gone on to choreograph and perform alongside Miley Cyrus in the iconic 2015 MTV VMA performance, which starred over 30 drag performers, and in 2018 she tore up the floor as a contestant on *So You Think You Can Dance*, making it through to the top 33 – yas gawd!

Laila McQueen

"I'm the crossbreed between a cute stripper and a punk rock girl."

Quick Stats

DRAG RACE:
Season 8

RANKING:
11th/12th place

SIGNATURE LOOK:
Glam Goth Realness

TYPE:
The #DeathSplat Queen

**FAN-FAVOURITE
PERFORMANCE:**
"Tainted Love" by Marilyn Manson

What's the T?

Performing her first official drag gig the day after she turned 18, Gloucester, Massachusetts' Laila McQueen (Tyler Devlin) spent her high school years building her drag skill set in art projects and rebelliously cross-dressing at parties. A self-proclaimed "bra and panties with a blazer" queen with a rabid lesbian fanbase, Laila appeared in the eighth season of *Drag Race* where she found herself in the bottom two in the first two episodes of the season, finally being eliminated in the shocking double elimination to "I Will Survive" with Dax ExclamationPoint. Following her time on the *Race*, Laila has worked with WOWPresents, creating makeup tutorial videos as well as viral content alongside previous *Drag Race* contestants.

LaShauwn
Beyond

"This is not RuPaul's Best Friend Race!"

Quick Stats

DRAG RACE:
Season 4

RANKING:
12th place

SIGNATURE LOOK:
Out Of This World Hair Fantasy
Realness

TYPE:
The Seamstress Queen

**FAN-FAVOURITE
PERFORMANCE:**
"Radio" by Beyoncé

What's the T?

Coining one of the most famous lines of *Drag Race* doesn't happen every day, but for LaShauwn Beyond it's only the tip of the impact this queen has made on the world of drag. Prior to her appearance on *Drag Race*'s fourth season, LaShauwn Beyond was well known as a costumier and seamstress from Florida who had previously worked for Season 4 sister Latrice Royale, creating sickening custom gowns. Despite turning out a sky-scraping "post apopkalakic" look in the first costume challenge, LaShauwn found herself eliminated after the wrestling challenge, which proved to be a feat too difficult for the seamstress extraordinaire. Following the *Race*, LaShauwn Beyond spends more of her time behind the scenes turning out epic costumes, prom gowns and gag-worthy looks for stars like makeup guru Patrick Starrr. Her Instagram account is to die for and a must for any lover of a nude illusion!

Latrice Royale

"She is large and in charge. Chunky yet funky."

Quick Stats

DRAG RACES:
Season 4 | *All Stars* 1 | *All Stars* 4

RANKING:
4th place (Miss Congeniality) |
7th/8th place | 5th place (originally 7th)

POST DRAG RACE:
Introduced and performed "You Make Me Feel (Mighty Real)" with Jennifer Hudson at Fashion Rocks; released dance singles "Weight" (2014) and "Excuse the Beauty" (2018); officiates weddings and civil ceremonies as a certified marriage celebrant; released a jazz EP *Here's to Life: Latrice Royale Live in the Studio*

SIGNATURE LOOK:
Diamante Diva Realness

TYPE:
The Large and in Charge Queen

FAN-FAVOURITE PERFORMANCE:
"Weight" (Season 7 Grand Finale) by Latrice Royale

What's the T?

Raised in Compton, California, Timothy Wilcots' drag persona Latrice Royale emerged in the mid 1990s at the Fort Lauderdale club The Copa, where she won her first amateur drag contest. A natural performer with an incredible work ethic and captivating moves, Latrice competed in the pageant circuit winning the title of Miss Pride South Florida in 2004.

Latrice Royale won the hearts of fans across the globe after her performance on the fourth season of *Drag Race*. By not only being a "B.I.T.C.H." (Being in Total Control of Herself) but also a formidable costumier, performer and all-round polished queen, Latrice powered her way to the top four of the competition and won the title of Miss Congeniality. Lip sync performances against Kenya Michaels – "(You Make Me Feel) Like a Natural Woman" – and DiDa Ritz – "I've Got to Use My Imagination" – demonstrated a world-class style of classic drag artistry. In the months following, Latrice teamed up to form "Team Latrila" with Manila Luzon in the first season of *All Stars*, bringing back her timeless wit and warmth to the screen as a fan-favourite. After the fourth season of *Drag Race*, Royale founded talent management firm All Starr Management and even went on to star in the Logo TV documentary *Gays in Prison* (2015), where she discussed her life behind bars prior to her appearance on *Drag Race*.

Almost seven years after her initial appearance on *Drag Race*, Latrice Ru-turned to the competition in the fourth season of *All Stars* handcuffed to her *All Stars* 1 teammate Manila Luzon. Though an eternally fierce and beloved queen, Latrice found herself eliminated twice (fun fact: she's the only queen to be eliminated four times ever!) after less than fabulous performances in the "Jersey Justice" and "Sex and the Kitty, Girl 3" comedy challenges. Though the crown slipped away from her again, Latrice delivered old-school class and professionalism to the competition, continuing to teach the children to stay fierce and above all love each other!

Lineysha Sparx

"So fierce, so flawless, so sparkling!"

Quick Stats

DRAG RACE:
Season 5

RANKING:
9th place

SIGNATURE LOOK:
Miss Puerto Rico Realness

TYPE:
The Latina Glamazon

FAN-FAVOURITE PERFORMANCE:
"Whine Up" by Kat DeLuna

What's the T?

One of the most glamorous Puerto Rican queens to grace the main stage of *RuPaul's Drag Race*, Lineysha Sparx (Andy Trinidad), happens to also be one of the most appreciated queens out of drag as well... as far as trade is concerned! From the outset of Season 5, Lineysha demonstrated a masterful ability to create costumes out of almost anything, with her wallpaper couture receiving a rapturous response from the judges in the first episode. As the season went on, Lineysha's style and runway presentations wowed, but the language barrier that affected her Puerto Rican sisters on previous seasons caught up with her and sent her packing after a lacklustre Celia Cruz impersonation on the "Snatch Game". Still a young queen with a bright future, Lineysha continues to entertain audiences across the United States with her Latin glamour.

DRAG TERM

Halleloo

An interjection to express happiness or praise, like
"hallelujah", and much like "yass!" or "werk!", this
term is used by drag queens and gay men alike
today. If you've caught any of Season 3 you will
have heard the word used at least
once by Shangela.

Heather

The opposite of a "booger", a "heather" is a way
of describing a queen who is polished and fierce.
In Season 3 "The Heathers" alliance consisted
of Raja, Delta Work, Carmen Carrera and Manila
Luzon – queens who self-identified as the
strongest competitors in that *Race* due to their
strengths in style, performance and all-round
drag artistry.

Madame LaQueer

"Are we talking about beavers or... ewwwwwwwww!"

Quick Stats

DRAG RACE:
Season 4

RANKING:
10th place

SIGNATURE LOOK:
80s Villainess Realness

TYPE:
The Fierce Face Queen

FAN-FAVOURITE PERFORMANCE:
"Lean On Medley" by Major Lazer
& Various

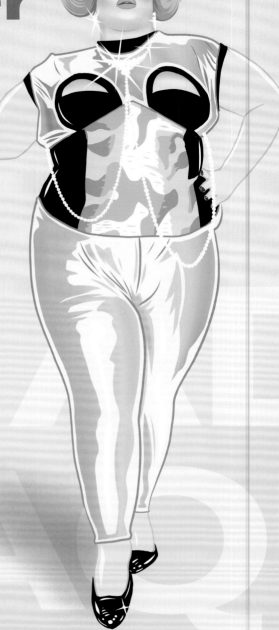

What's the T?

Since commencing her drag career at the start of the new millennium, Madame LaQueer (Carlos Melendez) has built a drag empire of her own in Puerto Rico: producing shows, winning four pageants, and launching the careers of queens like fellow Racers April Carrión and Kandy Ho at her event *Queen of the Night*. Appearing in Season 4 of *Drag Race*, Madame won the "WTF! Wrestling's Trashiest Fighters" challenge at the start of the season with teammate Chad Michaels, but soon found herself in the bottom two after a poor performance in the acting challenge. Turning it out as a "pointer sister" performer ("pointer sisters are the girls who just point during a lip sync..." – Jiggly Caliente) to Pink's "Trouble", LaQueer was sent packing by Milan. Inspired to move to Southern California after her time on *Drag Race*, Madame LaQueer continues to entertain fans at famous drag spot Micky's in WeHo.

Magnolia Crawford

"I'm just here for the exposure."

Quick Stats

DRAG RACE:
Season 6

RANKING:
13th/14th place

SIGNATURE LOOK:
Blonde Bombshell Realness

TYPE:
The Misunderstood Queen

**FAN-FAVOURITE
PERFORMANCE:**
"No One Tells a Queen What To Do"
by Magnolia Crawford & Adam Barta

What's the T?

A jet-setting queen by trade, Magnolia Crawford (Reynolds Engelhart) is a conceptual queen who is – intentionally – stylistically stuck in the late 1980s/ early 1990s. The blonde bombshell who prefers to be seen on computer screens rather than live on stage, was unfortunately eliminated on the first episode of Season 6 of *Drag Race*, after a less than inspired cow-patterned costume presentation on the main stage. After being met with negative criticism after the appearance on *Drag Race*, Engelhart decided to give the character of Magnolia Crawford a break and focus on his career as a flight attendant.

Manila Luzon

"See – this is how you do drag girls!"

Quick Stats

DRAG RACES:
Season 3 | *All Stars* 1 | *All Stars* 4

RANKING:
2nd place | 7th/8th place | 6th place

POST DRAG RACE:
Star of *RuPaul's Drag Race* spin-offs *Drag U* and *Drag My Dinner Party* with Raven and Jujubee; released singles "Hot Couture" (2011), "Helen Keller" (with Cazwell) (2014) and "That's A Man Maury" (with Willam) (2017); featured in television advertisement "Red Ribbon Runway" raising awareness for HIV/AIDS

SIGNATURE LOOK:
Pineapple Couture Eleganza

TYPE:
The Filipino Fashionista

FAN-FAVOURITE PERFORMANCE:
"MacArthur Park" by Donna Summer

What's the T?

After his first stint in drag as Cruella de Vil at 19, Karl Westerberg created Manila Luzon in the late 2000s as he appeared in the New York night life as a club queen with partner and *Drag Race* legend Sahara Davenport.

Appearing in the third season of *Drag Race*, Luzon blitzed her way ahead of the competition in iconic couture, ranging from Big Bird cosplay to pineapple ball gown realness. The winner of three main challenges and member of the feisty Heathers troupe, Luzon's strong work ethic and blend of glamour and camp pushed her to the top two of the contest, surrendering the crown to Raja. Her iconic performance of Donna Summer's "MacArthur Park" against Delta Work remains one of the strongest Lip Sync for Your Life performances in the herstory of the show.

In the years following, Manila became one of the first queens to release her own music as well as starring as a playable character in the iPhone App drag game *Dragopolis*. Luzon has collaborated with fashion designers Viktor Luna (from *Project Runway*) as well as strutted catwalks for LA designer Marco Marco. Celebrating her iconic costumes, Manila has also released her first ever self-illustrated costume book, *Manila Luzon's Fineapple Couture*.

Galvanised and ready to take the crown in her third attempt, Luzon was cast in *All Stars* 4 where she brought to the competition a skill set any other competitor would envy. Winning three challenges in a row and establishing herself as "the one to beat", Luzon found herself in the firing line on her first landing in the bottom two of the competition with both Monét X Change and Naomi Smalls choosing the lipstick to eliminate Manila should they win the Lip Sync for Your Legacy. In what many say is the most cunning act in *Drag Race* herstory, Naomi's elimination of Manila in *All Stars* 4 rocked the competition and the fandom, but Manila rose above the shade to return to the world an eternally fierce double All Star with a legion of well over 1 million followers worldwide.

Mariah

"When it comes to going out in drag in the day time, I'm good... if it's right, it's right."

Quick Stats

DRAG RACE:
Season 3

RANKING:
9th place

SIGNATURE LOOK:
Feathered Fish Realness

TYPE:
The Ballroom Queen

FAN-FAVOURITE PERFORMANCE:
"Your Body" by Christina Aguilera

What's the T?

Born from the hallowed ground that is the ballroom scene of Atlanta, Mariah Paris Balenciaga (Elijah Kelly) – referred to only as Mariah during her appearance – created her mystifying drag persona while working as a top celebrity hair stylist. Having "brought it to the ball" differently with each contest back home, Mariah was more than ready for the challenges of Season 3, even though she hadn't much experience performing in actual drag shows. Serving not only a fierce sense of style and "mug4dayz" (the name of Mariah's first dance single – as well as her Insta handle) on the show, but a slick sense of wit, Mariah worked her way to the middle of the pack after a stumble in the "Snatch Game" as a less than fierce Joan Crawford. Following the *Race*, Mariah moved to LA to become a bonafide star of the West Hollywood drag scene, teaching the children how to nail their first time at a ball as a professor on *RuPaul's Drag U* and appearing on countless WOWPresents series such as *Fashion Photo RuView* and *Wait, What?* with Kimora Blac.

Max

"I'm Max – a starlet on the rise!"

Quick Stats

DRAG RACE:
Season 7

RANKING:
9th place

SIGNATURE LOOK:
Sultry in Steel Realness

TYPE:
The Silver Screen Beauty Queen

**FAN–FAVOURITE
PERFORMANCE:**
"I Put a Spell On You" from *Hocus Pocus*

What's the T?

Meeting at the cross-section of old Hollywood and Iggy Azalea, the silver-haired seductress of Season 7, Max Malanaphy took her first steps in drag in 2012 as Dr Frank N. Furter in a Minneapolis production of *The Rocky Horror Show*. In the following years, Max dialled up the vamp to 11 as her drag persona morphed into the vintage vixen that appeared on *Drag Race* – wowing audiences with not only killer ensembles (her "Bleeding Heart" runway slays!) but an entrancing disposition that saw her soar through the competition. While failing to bring the laughs (and the "boos") with her impression of Sharon Needles in the "Snatch Game", Max found herself eliminated after a lip sync against Jaidynn Diore Fierce. Looking at her time on the *Race* as an audition for a future in drag, Max has continued to perform and serve up flawless looks for her Instagram fans.

MAX

Mayhem Miller

"Guess who finally decided to crash the party?"

Quick Stats

DRAG RACE:
Season 10

RANKING:
10th place

SIGNATURE LOOK:
Chocolate Judd Realness

TYPE:
The Party Queen

FAN-FAVOURITE PERFORMANCE:
"Killing Me Softly (Live)" by Fugees

What's the T?

Starting drag on the very same night (May 10, 2002) as her *Drag Race* sisters Raven and Morgan McMichaels, Mayhem Miller (Dequan Johnson) has worked stages near and far to become one of the most beloved and iconic performers in the Southern California scene. A well-rounded queen and show producer from Riverside, whose singing chops are as polished as her mug, Mayhem auditioned for every season since Season 2 before she was finally cast to fans' excitement in the 10th season of *Drag Race*. Known at home as the Queen of the Party, Mayhem turned it out for the "Drag on a Dime" challenge, taking home the win for her latex glove eleganza, but found herself in the bottom after fading into the background during the "Tap That App" challenge. Outshone by Miz Cracker's Dr Dill character in "The Bossy Rossy Show" challenge, Mayhem was eliminated far earlier than both fans and she expected after the long eight years she spent hoping to be cast. While Season 10 may not have been Mayhem Miller's time to shine (come on *All Stars*!) she's turned parties across the world since *Drag Race* and has even appeared in sister Blair St. Clair's music video for "Call My Life".

Milan

"Colored Girl, why your base look like chalk?!"

Quick Stats

DRAG RACE:
Season 4

RANKING:
9th place

SIGNATURE LOOK:
Janelle Monae Realness

TYPE:
The Broadway Queen

FAN-FAVOURITE PERFORMANCE:
"The Miss Cleo Song" by Dwayne Milan

What's the T?

An accomplished actor, singer/songwriter and dancer in New York City prior to her appearance on Season 4, Milan (Dwayne Cooper) had not only starred in *Hairspray* on Broadway, but had gone viral with her 2006 parody video Miss Cleo, which garnered over 1.5 million views on YouTube. Through three Lip Sync for Your Life contests, audiences were wowed by Milan's high-energy performance style as she "swiffered the floor with her taint", flipped wigs and vogued on her head like no contestant before. Performing as Milan has taken a backseat, but the consummate triple-threat Dwayne has continued his performance on stage and screen in *Unbreakable Kimmy Schmidt* and 2017's musical tour of *The Doo Wop Project*.

House

In ballroom culture, a house is a group of individuals who operate as a surrogate family for young queer people, often those who are black or Latino, estranged from their biological families and struggling to survive. The House of LaBeija is said to be the very first house founded in the early 1970s with house "mother" Crystal LaBeija leading this group to outdo all other houses in order to reign supreme.

DRAG TERM

The house down

A phrase used at the end of sentences to describe "a lot" or a great amount; a very drawn out exclamation point. For example: "Trinity Taylor can dance the house down" (Trinity can dance!). "The house down" can be followed by other words like "boots" to draw out the strength of the exclamation.

Milk

"Milk! She does a body good, girl."

Quick Stats

DRAG RACES:
Season 6 | *All Stars* 3

RANKING:
9th place | 9th place

POST DRAG RACE:
Star of her own World of Wonder produced web series *Milk's LegenDAIRY Looks*; coverboy for *Hello Mr.* magazine and a story entitled "Dan Donigan: Meet the Milk Man"; modelled in the Marc Jacobs Spring/Summer 2016 and Vivienne Westwood S/S 2018 campaigns

SIGNATURE LOOK:
Club-Kid Chameleon Realness

TYPE:
The Creative Clown

FAN-FAVOURITE PERFORMANCE:
"E.T. (Take Me Home)" by Cash Cash ft. Bebe Rexha

What's the T?

In 2008 ex-competitive figure skater Daniel Donigan, inspired by his new boyfriend and friends' impromptu "10-minute-makeover" drag, made his first ever drag transformation – a gender-fuck "Little Merman" fusion of male and female attire with a killer heel. Addicted to online makeup tutorials, Milk was soon born after a move to NYC where she was immediately snatched up by nightlife icon Susanne Bartsch – an old friend of RuPaul and the 90s club-kids. Pumping out week after week of offbeat yet high-fashion looks, Milk and her drag posse the Dairy Queens took the New York drag scene by storm with their incomparable theme-oriented conceptual style of drag. Milk's *Drag Race* audition tape was a rainbow wheel of innovative looks, comedic schtick and fresh creativity not seen before on the *Race* runway. Entering the werkroom a statuesque flamenco-themed glamazon clown, Milk set the bar for her soon to be legendary looks, which included her take on Pinocchio, JonBenét Ramsey realness, RuPaul (the werkroom male Ru that is!) and the envelope-pushing bearded Gandalf moment in episode 1's runway. Expectedly punished by Michelle Visage's "When Will You Show Us Glamour" shtick week in week out, Milk never succumbed to pressure to tame her creativity, honouring her own sense of glamour and fabulousness until an untimely elimination in the sixth week of the competition. Milk's immense popularity following Season 6 made her a prime choice for *All Stars* 3 and while her runways showed great evolution in her drag aesthetic, she unfortunately found herself eliminated early in the competition after stumbles in the musical and comedy challenges.

Milk's modelling work has gone from strength to strength since her time on *Drag Race*, with not only campaigns for Marc Jacobs and Vivienne Westwood under her belt, but she appeared as the face of the MDNA Skin (yep, that's Madonna's skin care range!) campaign in 2017 as Madonna herself, circa the Blond Ambition Tour.

Mimi Imfurst

"Boo just 'cause you got a sugar daddy who pays everything for you..."

Quick Stats

DRAG RACES:
Season 3 | *All Stars* 1

RANKING:
11th place | 11th/12th place

SIGNATURE LOOK:
Lady DJ Realness

TYPE:
The Theatre Queen

FAN-FAVOURITE PERFORMANCE:
"The Roast of Michelle Visage" by Mimi Imfurst

What's the T?

An insult comic extraordinaire with a long career as a DJ, hostess, theatre and drag performer, Mimi Imfurst (Braden Chapman) is "Jill of all trades" when it comes to the performing arts game. While a popular working New York queen before Season 3, Mimi famously found herself in hot water with fellow contestants and the rabid *Drag Race* fanbase as she (literally) picked up India Ferrah and threw the insults back at Shangela, in what are now iconic moments of the series. Such scenes led to her casting in the first season of *All Stars* where the drama continued in the form of hostility from her teammate Pandora Boxx, leading to an early elimination. Following her two explosive *Drag Race* appearances, Mimi Imfurst has found great success on the pageant circuit, winning the title of Miss'd America (2016) and as a show producer creating the famous Battle of the Seasons and Dragapalooza live concert tours. In 2018 Mimi returned to the stage in the 20th anniversary of *Hedwig and the Angry Inch* in the titular role, adding the production's soundtrack to her growing discography of gems, which include her debut album *The Fire*, parody singles and hits with girl group XELLE.

Miss Fame

"Greetings Earth Queens, I come in peace"

Quick Stats

DRAG RACE:
Season 7

RANKING:
7th place

SIGNATURE LOOK:
Rubber Doll Realness

TYPE:
The Macquillage Mistress of Drag

**FAN-FAVOURITE
PERFORMANCE:**
"Primitive" by Richard Vission vs.
Luciana

What's the T?

Working as a well-respected makeup artist and editorial model for years before her appearance on the seventh season of *Drag Race*, Miss Fame (Kurtis Dam-Mikkelsen) entered the *Race* as a fan-favourite with her out-of-this-world aesthetic. The self-proclaimed "Rolls Royce of Drag" brought to the show not only a slew of sickening makeup and costume creations, but revealed her country side – winning audiences over with her goofy and loveable personality before an elimination lip sync against Pearl in the "Divine Inspiration" runway challenge. Immediately after her time on the show, Miss Fame took the challenge of taking her brand to new heights by not only releasing her debut solo record *Beauty Marked* (2015) and touring her makeup tutorials across the United States, but by forging an unprecedented relationship with L'Oréal as a spokesmodel, where she walked the 2016 Cannes Film Festival red carpet as the first drag artist ever to grace that event. In 2018 Miss Fame unleashed at DragCon her first ever makeup collection – Miss Fame Beauty – kickstarting a new universe of ventures for our cosmic queen of glamour.

MISS
FAME

Miz Cracker

"I'm thin, I'm white and I'm very salty. And that's what makes me a cracker"

Quick Stats

DRAG RACE:
Season 10

RANKING:
5th place

SIGNATURE LOOK:
Jewish Barbie Realness

TYPE:
The Saltine Queen

FAN-FAVOURITE PERFORMANCE:
"Whip It/Whip My Hair/Whip It Medley" by Devo, Willow Smith & Nicki Minaj

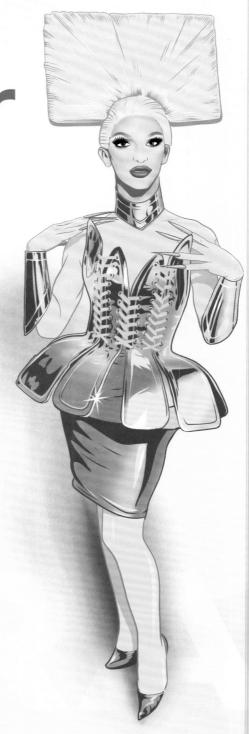

What's the T?

After a chance encounter helping a stranger in the New York City snow – who turned out to be Bob the Drag Queen! – Miz Cracker (Maxwell Heller) found herself immersed in her new friend's world of wigs and costumes and ultimately pressured by Bob to give drag a shot in 2011. Participating in Bob's weekly wedding ceremonies in Times Square protesting for LGBTQ+ marriage equality, Miz Cracker caught the bug and found herself working to improve her drag week after week, trying out looks in the local club scene before honing her craft and starting her full-blown career as a drag comedienne. Cast alongside four other New York-based queens in Season 10 of *Drag Race*, Cracker found herself immediately pitted against young starlet Aquaria, with rumours of the queens copying each other's looks causing early drama in the competition. Winning over audiences with not only her polished runway presentations and shelarious comedy stylings, Miz Cracker's personal stories of growing up impoverished allowed for her vulnerability to show. Snatching a win in the makeover challenge where she made over YouTuber Chester See into the pretty in pink icon Miz Cookie, Cracker soon found herself eliminated by lip sync assassin Kameron Michaels. A fan-favourite, Miz Cracker has wasted no time in keeping her fans wanting more after the *Race*, appearing in the Billboard web series *Spillin' the Tea* with Tammie Brown and Jasmine Masters and in her own WOWPresents web series *JewTorials*.

Monét X Change

"I'm Monét X Change and you better get your currency in check, bitch"

Quick Stats

DRAG RACES:
Season 10 | *All Stars* 4

RANKING:
6th place (Miss Congeniality) |
Winner

SIGNATURE LOOK:
Spongebob Eleganza Extravaganza

TYPE:
The Pusscat Coifed Comedy Queen

**FAN-FAVOURITE
PERFORMANCE:**
"Pound the Alarm" by Nicki Minaj

What's the T?

New York City-born performing arts student Monét X Change (Kevin Bertin) got the itch to try out the art of drag after attending a drag ball where the legendary Peppermint performed, culminating in her first drag outing in Pride 2012.

Working the bar scene solidly for several years before her big break, Monét's honest and electric performance style won over the tough New York crowds and even nabbed her a pageant crown – queen of Gay Caribbean USA 2014. Jump forward four years and this NY favourite was cast in the 10th season of *RuPaul's Drag Race* where she placed high for most of the competition keeping audiences gagging on her comedy in the "Snatch Game" as Maya Angelou and in the "Breastworld" challenge. Delivering both sickening and questionable runway presentations, it was Monét's iconic sponge dress from the "Drag on a Dime" challenge that became her trademark of the season and after her elimination at the hands of Kameron Michaels. Although eliminated earlier than fans had hoped, Monét was able to nab Season 10's Miss Congeniality crown, as voted by her fellow contestants, setting her up for a mighty return in *All Stars* 4.

Monét X Change returned to the *All Stars* competition ready to prove to audiences her strengths as an entertainer, but also demonstrate growth in her style. Nabbing wins in performance ("Super Girl Groups, Henny"), comedy (the Lady Bunny Roast) and in the makeover challenge, Monet proved she was one of the queens to beat, pushing her into a finale where her Wakanda-inspired "Super Queen" performance and final lip sync against Trinity The Tuck earned her a place alongside Trinity in the Drag Race Hall of Fame. Not one to wait, Monét dropped her visual EP *Unapologetically* following her win, demonstrating that the sponge queen we once knew has a brand new style and sound – so you better soak it up!

Monica Beverly Hillz

"Who you callin' ghetto?"

Quick Stats

DRAG RACE:
Season 5

RANKING:
12th place

SIGNATURE LOOK:
Fish From The Block Realness

TYPE:
The Banjee Babe

**FAN-FAVOURITE
PERFORMANCE:**
"Hot Sugar" by Tamar Braxton

What's the T?

Before appearing in the fifth season of *Drag Race*, Chicago's Monica Beverly Hillz had spent seven years building her drag persona, inspired by her love for dance and her passion for the fun and flirty side of the art form. Serving straight-up banjee girl realness in her runway performances and backstage in her Untucked spat with Serena ChaCha, it was the "Draggle Rock" challenge which challenged Monica's acting abilities and saw her sashay away. Just prior to her elimination, Monica bravely came out – not only to her fellow contestants and the judges, but the world – as transgender, educating audiences that "trans is who (she is) and drag is what (she does)". Following her time on the *Race*, Monica Beverly Hillz joined her *Drag Race* sisters onstage with Miley Cyrus at the VMA awards, continues to entertain in drag at clubs across the United States and uses her experience with transitioning to inform and educate in online editorials and YouTube interviews.

Monique Heart

"Facts are facts!"

Quick Stats

DRAG RACES:
Season 10 | *All Stars* 4

RANKING:
8th place | Co-runner Up

SIGNATURE LOOK:
Brown Cow Stunning Couture

TYPE:
The Heart of Season 10

**FAN-FAVOURITE
PERFORMANCE:**
"No Tears Left To Cry/Sorry Not Sorry
Medley" by Ariana Grande &
Demi Lovato

What's the T?

Kansas City's Monique Heart (Kevin Richardson) quickly went from newly out gay boy on the scene in March 2011 to a fully fledged drag queen in October that same year. Inspired by the drag performers who were pillars in her community, Monique (who is also a minister!) combined her faith and passion for drag artistry to quickly rise in the ranks within her scene in Missouri, becoming a quick-witted host of drag bingo.

Voguing her way into the Season 10 werkroom, Monique Heart hit it off with fans and her competitors alike, giving strong performances in "The Bossy Rossy Show" and "Drag on a Dime" challenges. Unfortunately her last minute mermaid runway and poor performance as politician Maxine Waters in the "Snatch Game" landed Monique Heart in the bottom two against The Vixen. Failing to remember the words to Carly Rae Jepsen's "Cut to the Feeling", Monique dropped and rolled across the main stage off both the set and the *Race*. Following Season 10, Monique toured the world and joined the cast of The Vixen's *Black Girl Magic* alongside Season 10 sisters Mayhem Miller and Monét X Change before returning to screens in the fourth season of *All Stars*.

Emerging from the gate a queen with a point to prove, Monique brought a (brown cow) stunning new wardrobe and attitude to the competition, delivering shelarious performances in the "Jersey Justice" and "Sex and the Kitty, Girl 3" challenges. Winning three challenges and proving to audiences that she is a fierce "Super Queen" on both the runway and in challenges, Monique Heart powered through to place as runner up alongside Naomi Smalls. The heart of Season 10 and *All Stars* 4 has just given the world a taste of the "ooh ah ah sensation", but what can fans expect from her next?

DRAG TERM

Judy

A Judy, or "good Judy", is a way to describe a gay male you would consider a very good or close friend. The term "Judy" originates from the gay slang "friend of Dorothy" – a euphemism for "gay", dating back as far as World War II. Dorothy in *The Wizard of Oz* was, of course, played by Judy Garland, thus signalling the evolution of the term over time.

Kaikai

The act of sex between two drag queens.
Often used to describe the act while both parties
are dressed in drag, the term can also be used
for drag queens hooking up out of drag as well.
For example: "I know she's my sister but she's hot,
so we decided to kaikai last night instead of
finding trade".

Morgan McMichaels

"You have no class and no manners... so go fix your hair, go fix your mug"

Quick Stats

DRAG RACES:
Season 2 | *All Stars* 3

RANKING:
8th place | 5th place (originally 10th)

SIGNATURE LOOK:
#Booty4Dayz Realness

TYPE:
The Inimitable Queen of Performance

FAN-FAVOURITE PERFORMANCE:
"If I Were a Boy" by Beyoncé

What's the T?

West Hollywood icon Morgan McMichaels (Thomas White) started her drag career in 2002, curating a persona with an impeccable skill set of dance ability, makeup artistry and untouchable impersonation – inspired by and under the guidance of drag mother Chad Michaels. Entering the second season of *Drag Race* as a seasoned performer with best friend Raven, Morgan was one to beat as she won the first "Gone with the Windows" costume challenge and gave a shelarious performance as an eccentric grandmother in the "Country Queens" Disco Extra Greasy Shortening commercial challenge. After a stumble in the "Snatch Game" as an aesthetically correct – yet stiff-as-a-board – Pink, and two power-packed lip syncs, Morgan found herself eliminated a lot earlier than fans anticipated.

 In the years after *Drag Race*, Morgan starred as a professor in the *Drag Race* spin-off *Drag U* and appeared in her own WOWPresents web series *Living for the Lip Sync*. Cast in the third season of *RuPaul's Drag Race All Stars*, Morgan entered guns blazing, announcing that she wouldn't hesitate to eliminate her strongest competition. Unfortunately Morgan spoke too soon and found herself ousted first off the rank after a lip sync performance to her debut single "Why You Mad Tho?" by BenDeLaCreme, who brought her back into the competition following the "Handmaids to Kitty Girls" challenge only to be eliminated again the following week. Morgan McMichaels continues to spend her time solidifying her career as one of the most fierce queens in WeHo, cementing Monday nights at Micky's as the epicentre of drag on the West Coast.

Mystique Summers Madison

"Bitch I am from Chicago!"

Quick Stats

DRAG RACE:
Season 2

RANKING:
10th place

SIGNATURE LOOK:
Two Piece and a Biscuit Realness

TYPE:
The #Painted4Filth Diva

**FAN-FAVOURITE
PERFORMANCE:**
"Work It/Gossip Folks" by Missy Elliott

What's the T?

The original large and in charge *Drag Race* diva from the South, Mystique Summers Madison (Donté Sims) started performing in drag in 2005 and while competing in the Imperial Court pageant system, won the title of North Carolina All American Goddess. With several pageants under her belt, Mystique was cast on Season 2 ready and thirsty to take the crown representing the big girls, serving Southern glamour and charm. While winning the "Country Queens" Chicken, or What? challenge, Mystique found herself in the bottom two after a less than impressive "mall drag" interpretation of country realness – and sashayed away in a stage-splitting fierce exit. In the following years after her season of *Drag Race*, Mystique still performs in drag, touring the seas with the Al and Chuck Drag Stars at Sea cruises and has appeared in various WOWPresents viral videos.

Naomi Smalls

"Check your lipstick before you come for me!"

Quick Stats

DRAG RACES:
Season 8 | *All Stars* 4

RANKING:
Co-runner Up | Co-runner Up

SIGNATURE LOOK:
90s Supermodel Realness

TYPE:
The High-fashion Hood Rat

FAN–FAVOURITE PERFORMANCE:
"Roses" by ABRA

What's the T?

Spending her junior years of high school watching *Drag Race*, Naomi Smalls (Davis Heppenstall) is truly a new-generation queen who has grown with the *Race* as inspiration for her artistry and performance style. Winning Raven's Raucous Roundup Drag Competition in Pomona in 2013, Naomi made the decision to follow her mentor and participate in the eighth season of the *Race* as one of the youngest competitors that cycle. Bringing her brand of supermodel meets Studio 54 glamour to the runway, Naomi Smalls took out a top three position serving sickening runway presentations including her challenge-winning – now iconic – "Wizards of Drag" scarecrow look. Naomi's performance of her final three track "Legs" wowed the audiences at the reunion and boasts over 1.5 million views on YouTube today!

Following Season 8, Naomi Smalls starred alongside *Race*-mate Kim Chi in their makeup review series *M.U.G.* and in 2018 started to chronicle her worldwide touring serving 90s VHS tape realness in YouTube series *Small's World*. Ready to burn the *All Stars* 4 runway, Naomi spent the opening weeks of the season flying under the radar, delivering sickening runways that spoke to her style eye and evolution since her first time in the *Race* as a 21-year-old. Determined to stand out from the pack following a Cher-tastic win in the makeover challenge with her best Judy, and an even more epic lip sync to Judy Garland's "Come Rain or Come Shine", Naomi Smalls delivered the greatest gag of the season by eliminating the front runner and fan-favourite Manila Luzon. Naomi's warning shots to her fellow competitors rocked the competition and demonstrated that she has the nerve to match her style, which pushed her through to place runner up alongside Monique Heart. A style queen for the age, celebrating the androgyny of Prince and the glamour of the 50s housewife with a dash of Studio 54 dazzle, Naomi is a young yet polished entertainer with leg-endary career ahead of her!

Naysha Lopez

"Hola! The beauty
is here!"

Quick Stats

DRAG RACE:
Season 8

RANKING:
9th place (originally 12th)

SIGNATURE LOOK:
Pageant Princesa Realness

TYPE:
#TheBeauty

**FAN-FAVOURITE
PERFORMANCE:**
"Miss DragCon Pageant
Medley" by Various

What's the T?

A Chicago queen with an accomplished Latin dance career, Naysha Lopez (Fabian Rodriguez) spent the 13 years of her drag career before the *Race* slaying the stage and snatching crowns including the prestigious title of Miss Continental 2013. With a title that has been shared with the likes of icons Candis Cayne and Erica Andrews, Naysha entered Season 8 of *RuPaul's Drag Race* as a contestant to watch out for – but soon found herself eliminated in the first episode after a poor effort creating a look in the style of Season 1's "Drag on a Dime" thrift store-based design challenge. After a swift phone call from RuPaul following a double elimination, this "rectangle girl of the world" returned to the competition for two more weeks before sashaying away for a second time following her less than groovy "Dragometry" live performance. Although not an America's Next Drag Superstar, Naysha Lopez has returned to taking home pageant trophies – including scoring the title of Miss New York Universo Latina USA 2017 – and continuing to tour "the beauty" across the United States.

Nicole
Paige
Brooks

"You know you want a taste of cherry pie!"

Quick Stats

DRAG RACE:
Season 2

RANKING:
11th place

SIGNATURE LOOK:
Southern Fish Realness

TYPE:
The Fan-Favourite Diva of Atlanta, Georgia

FAN-FAVOURITE PERFORMANCE:
"Shake It Off" by Taylor Swift

What's the T?

The seductive Southern belle with charm that's sweeter than the taste of her cherry pie and as sharp as her acrylic toenails for days, Nicole Paige Brooks (Bryan Christopher Pryor), from Atlanta, Georgia, began her successful career as a performer at 21 as part of a Halloween dare like many queens before her. Determined to improve her female impersonation act, Nicole was taken under the wing of drag mother Shawnna Brooks and her house, where she built the seasoned performer who appeared on the second season of *Drag Race*. A drag dad alongside *Race*-mate Tyra Sanchez, Nicole went into the *Race* with the goal of openly showing her son the career path that his dad had chosen, but was unfortunately eliminated in the second episode after a less than impressive "drunk Janice Dickinson-esque" strip show performance. The legend of Nicole Paige Brooks from Atlanta, Georgia, continues to echo in the hearts of Drag Racers and fans alike, as she continues to bring her self-proclaimed "X-Rated" brand of drag to nightclubs across the South and in videos on the WOWPresents network.

Nina Bo'Nina Brown

"Sue me!"

Quick Stats

DRAG RACE:
Season 9

RANKING:
6th place

SIGNATURE LOOK:
Face Paint Fantasy Realness

TYPE:
The Papercraft Queen

**FAN-FAVOURITE
PERFORMANCE:**
"Cola (Medley)" by Lana Del Rey

What's the T?

Inspired by cartoons, video games and her love for larger-than-life booty pads, Nina Bo'Nina (Banana Fofana Osama Bin Laden) Brown (Pierre Leverne Dease) challenges the definition of African–American queer identity and has brought to Atlanta an original perspective on the art of drag with her papercraft creations. Entering the *Drag Race* werkroom of Season 9 with one of the most original aesthetics, Nina showcased an epic slew of looks that ranged from skeleton hooker to Lady-Gaga-meets-working-girl fantasy to her jaw dropping Georgia peach, which won her the first week's challenge. While her inner demons played with Nina's ability to get a foothold in the competition in the weeks to follow, she found herself winning lip sync after lip sync, demonstrating she has the performance chops to match the wild looks. After a stumble in the "Crew Better Work" makeover challenge, Nina Bo'Nina Brown sashayed away, promising to bring more of her epic makeover tutorials on YouTube to life and to educate those queens back home in Atlanta that Nina's brand of drag SLAYS!

Nina Flowers

"LOCAAAAAAA!"

Quick Stats

DRAG RACES:
Season 1 | *All Stars* 1

RANKING:
2nd place (Miss Congeniality)|
9th/10th place

POST DRAG RACE:
Spins internationally as one of the
most in-demand circuit DJs; released
house singles including "Loca" (2009)
and "I'm Feelin' Flowers" (2011); starred
in the music video for Adore Delano's
"I Look Fuckin' Cool" with Alaska

SIGNATURE LOOK:
All Star Androgyny Realness

TYPE:
The Genderfuck Queen

**FAN-FAVOURITE
PERFORMANCE:**
"Addicted to Bass" by Puretone

What's the T?

Hailing from Bayamón, Puerto Rico, Jorge Flores Sanchez started doing drag at 19 against strong resistance from his family. Inspired by German punk rock artist Nina Hagen, Flores took her name and created Nina Flowers – an androgynous enigma that took the Denver drag scene by storm in 2008. Inherently creative like her Puerto Rican drag sisters back home, Flowers entered a drag scene populated by pageant queens and a pre-*Drag Race* world where the scene was not as established or welcoming as it is today.

Winning the online vote for the very first season of *RuPaul's Drag Race*, a then unknown TV competition loosely based on *America's Next Top Model*, Nina Flowers was from the outset a visually and conceptually different queen from pageant queens like Rebecca Glasscock, character impersonators like Shannel and dancing queens like Jade. Her honesty, warmth and heart were set against her strong and tattooed exterior, making her such an original character that one not only rooted for in the competition but adored her creativity and style. Finishing second to the first winner BeBe Zahara Benet, Nina took the title of Miss Congeniality and went back home to Denver where her drag was welcomed with open arms for the first time.

Following her appearances on *Drag Race* and *All Stars*, Nina has taken the club scene by storm. A star of the monthly Drag Nation in Denver, Nina continues to push boundaries with her style of Drag DJ'ing, releasing club singles and remixes, propelling her into the world of electronic music production. Nina is also lucky enough to have May 29 declared "Nina Flowers Day" in recognition of her contribution to Denver's LGBT community.

Kiki

"Kiki" is a term to describe gossip, small talk, chatting, or a heart-to-heart conversation, and must never be confused with "kaikai"! As described by the Scissor Sisters, a "Kiki is a party for calming all nerves... sipping tea and dishing just deserts one may deserve".

DRAG TERM

Mug

A person's face. Queens considered strongest at "beating their mugs" include Raven, Miss Fame, Roxxxy Andrews, Milk and Raja.

Ongina

"My middle name is Ong and God didn't bless me with a certain 'ina'"

Quick Stats

DRAG RACE:
Season 1

RANKING:
5th place

SIGNATURE LOOK:
High Concept Couture Realness

TYPE:
The Bald Beauty Queen

FAN-FAVOURITE PERFORMANCE:
"Beautiful" by Christina Aguilera

What's the T?

LA-based queen with Filipino roots, Ongina (Ryan Ong Palao) was fascinated as a child with the American concept of Halloween and, on her 21st birthday, made her androgynous gender-bending debut in drag. Inspired by fashion and women's shoes, Ongina spent the next six years of her drag career building the bubbly personality and sharp style that was presented in the very first season of *Drag Race*. One of the original fan-favourites of the series, Ongina won both the Destiny's Child-flavoured "Girl Group" challenge and the emotional "M.A.C. Viva-Glam" challenge. Inspired by her own HIV diagnosis, which she tearfully revealed to the judges and the world, Ongina created an optimistic commercial for the M.A.C. cosmetics line, which won her the respect of audiences worldwide. After a stumble in the girl fighter makeover challenge Ongina was sent packing by BeBe Zahara Benet in an electric lip sync contest, but her pint-sized power and humility solidified her status as a legendary Racer. Since the *Race*, Ongina starred as one of the head professors on *RuPaul's Drag U* and continues to entertain in West California with her brand of high-fashion, emotive drag performance.

Pandora Boxx

"Anyone that's eaten my cherry pie raves about it."

Quick Stats

DRAG RACES:
Season 2 | *All Stars* 1

RANKING:
5th place (Miss Congeniality) |
11th/12th place

POST DRAG RACE:
Writes for the "Gay Voices" section
of the *Huffington Post*; released pop
singles including "Nice Car! (Shame
about Your Penis)" (2012) and "Oops I
Think I Pooped" (2018); starred in drag
comedy series *She's Living for This* in
2013; hosts YouTube web series *The
Pandora Boxx Show*

SIGNATURE LOOK:
Colourful Comedienne Realness

TYPE:
The Susan Lucci of Drag

**FAN-FAVOURITE
PERFORMANCE:**
"Let It Go (Frozen Medley)",
by Various Artists

What's the T?

Inspired by fellow New York queen Darienne Lake, Pandora Boxx – the drag persona of Michael Steck – appeared on the Rochester drag scene in the mid-90s. Boxx, a classically styled female impersonator with a comedic flair, first appeared on US television screens in 1997 in an episode of Ricki Lake hilariously entitled "Get a grip doll... you're too fat to be a drag queen". In 2009 Pandora Boxx was cast in the second season of *RuPaul's Drag Race*. Although her styling and aesthetic weren't to the taste of judge Santino Rice, Boxx won the hearts of fans through her camp schtick, killer impersonation of Carol Channing in the "Snatch Game" and her honest discussion about suicide and depression. Crowned Miss Congeniality, Pandora went on to star in several spin-offs of *Drag Race* including *All Stars* and *Drag U*, as well as starring as the host of *Pandora Boxx's Drag Center* – a web series where Boxx would recap newly released *Drag Race* episodes.

Following her season on *Drag Race* Pandora became the first well-known comedy queen of the franchise and went on to star in stand-up comedy specials, which have starred future contestant Bianca Del Rio and drag comedy legends Miss Coco Peru and Jackie Beat. Pandora has joined other *Race* alumni in releasing pop singles, including "Cooter!" (2011) and "Different" (2014). Still touring strongly with the Battle of the Seasons Tour as well as appearing on all of the Drag Race Cruises, Boxx maintains her status as one of the original fan-favourites, bringing her brand of camp and comedy across the globe.

Pearl

"Bitch, I'm from New York and you can wear fur in spring. 'K?"

Quick Stats

DRAG RACE:
Season 7

RANKING:
Co-runner Up

POST DRAG RACE:
Produced and released her own dance/techno album *Pleasure* in 2015; curated her own signature fragrance "Flazéda"; starred in the music video to Violet Chachki's single "Bettie"; Reached over 1 million followers on Instagram

SIGNATURE LOOK:
Stepford Wife Robot Realness

TYPE:
The Old Hollywood Club-Kid

FAN-FAVOURITE PERFORMANCE:
"Hotride" by The Prodigy

What's the T?

Originally from St Petersburg, Florida, Matthew James Lent began his drag career in Chicago as Pearl in 2012. A feast for the eyes, Pearl creates performances and high-fashion looks that meld both Hollywood glamour and electric club-kid aesthetics. Although a fairly new queen on the scene, Pearl has been lucky enough to curate her own eccentric queer club nights Pleasure and Pain for Pleasure. Pearl made her television debut on Season 7 of *RuPaul's Drag Race* in 2015. Executing intricately styled and aesthetically delicious looks on the main stage, Pearl was criticised for "falling asleep" throughout the competition. After a fire was lit under her by RuPaul for not making a splash like her fellow competitors, Pearl won two team-based main challenges with Max in a comedy hosting of the "DESPY Awards" and with Trixie Mattel in the "Conjoined Queens" challenge. Fighting off the early criticism, Pearl championed to come as co-runner up with Ginger Minj.

Following *Drag Race* Pearl released her debut self-produced techno/dance album *Pleasure*, which featured the single "Love Slave" and charted at #11 on the US Billboard Dance/Electronic Album chart. In addition, Pearl went on to team up with perfume company Xyrena to release the fragrance "Flazéda", to create her very own high-fashion art doll Vladonna, and to showcase unreal celebrity impersonation makeup tutorials on her YouTube channel – her Sarah Jessica Parker is out of this world!

Penny Tration

"Everybody likes a little Penny Tration."

Quick Stats

DRAG RACE:
Season 5

RANKING:
14th place

SIGNATURE LOOK:
Painted for the Gawds Realness

TYPE:
The Effervescent Emcee Queen

FAN-FAVOURITE PERFORMANCE:
"Car Wash" by Rose Royce

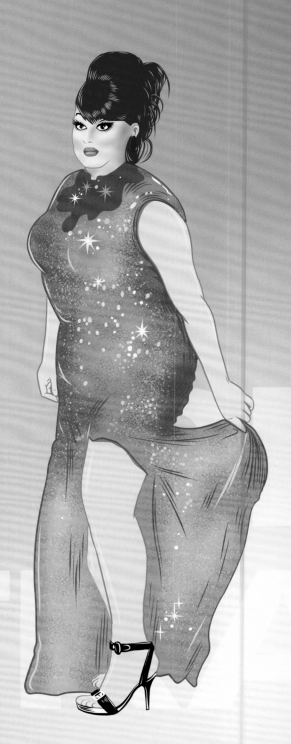

What's the T?

Inspired by the great Divine, Penny Tration (Tony Cody) started her career in drag over 20 years before her appearance on *Drag Race*, after encountering an entrancing performance by Louisville legend Hurricane Summers. An emcee extraordinaire and pageant winner with an fabulously old-school sense of wit and style, Penny was voted by the *Drag Race* Facebook fan community to be cast in Season 5 – and she was more than ready to bring her strong skill set to the competition. Presented with the challenge of dumpster diving for materials to create a unique piece of couture in the first challenge of the season, Penny was unable to put her fashion where her mouth was, and was sent home in a purple gown (which she later resurrected in her live reunion club-kid inspired costume). Following her time on the *Race*, Penny Tration has continued to compete in pageants, taking home the crown of Miss Ohio All American Goddess at Large 2014, and continuing to entertain crowds back home in Kentucky.

Peppermint

"The number one queen is
P–E–P–P–E–R-bitch,
you know the rest!"

Quick Stats

DRAG RACE:
Season 9

RANKING:
2nd place

SIGNATURE LOOK:
Candy Cane Club-kid Realness

TYPE:
The NYC Legend

**FAN-FAVOURITE
PERFORMANCE:**
"Servin' It Up" by Peppermint
ft. Cazwell

What's the T?

New York drag royalty with one heck of a sweet tooth, Miss Peppermint (Agnes Moore) has been turning parties since the late 1990s as a live performance queen who serves equal doses of fabulous and fierce. As a triple-threat singer, songwriter and dancer, Peppermint has not only released minty fresh club jams with NYC icons Cazwell and Sherry Vine, but her legacy is built on her congeniality and passion for performance. Peppermint's bubbly personality won over her fellow Racers and fans alike on Season 9, while her witty work on the Michelle Visage roast showed she can do sticky just as well as sweet. Though a few pink ensembles in her early runways left audiences wanting more, her club-kid couture stole the show and bolstered her journey to the crown. The undeniable lip sync assassin of her season, Peppermint's explosive wins over Cynthia Lee Fontaine and Alexis Michelle whet the audience's appetite for her Lip Sync for the Crown at the finale. While placing second, Peppermint is more than ready to take on the world with her brand of drag, which isn't measured by gender or boundaries, simply by fierceness!

Phi Phi O'Hara

"At least I am a showgirl, bitch, go back to Party City where you belong."

Quick Stats

DRAG RACES:
Season 4 | *All Stars* 2

RANKING:
Co-runner Up | 7th place

SIGNATURE LOOK:
Cosplay Chameleon Realness

TYPE:
The Showgirl-turned-Cosplay Queen

FAN-FAVOURITE PERFORMANCE:
"Anything You Can Do Medley"
by Various

What's the T?

A fierce queen who is not only a killer performer, live singer and makeup artist but also an inventive costume designer, Phi Phi O'Hara (Jaremi Carey) began her career as Lady Phoenix in 2004 prior to a move to Chicago and name change after joining the house of O'Hara under drag mother Asia O'Hara. A pageant winner prior to her time on Season 4, Phi Phi entered the competition with the crown in her sights, and her fiery desire to win that caused conflict – her rivalry with winner Sharon Needles making for some epic gay TV! Winning the "Dragazines" and "DILFs: Dads I'd Like to Frock" makeover challenges, Phi Phi made the top three of the contest. Later cast in *All Stars* 2, O'Hara's efforts to "Rudeem" herself for Season 4's shady behaviour fell short after blow ups with Alyssa Edwards and a Twitter tirade against RuPaul. While her time on both seasons weren't the best PR exercises for her brand, Phi Phi's immense talent hasn't been completely out-shadowed, as her "365 Days of Drag" Instagram project in 2016 solidified her status as an iconic queen of cosplay, not the "tired-ass showgirl" from years before.

Phoenix

"I can play well with others... But, I definitely do have a bitchy side!"

Quick Stats

DRAG RACE:
Season 3

RANKING:
12th place

SIGNATURE LOOK:
Lusciousness in a Leotard Realness

TYPE:
The Fiery Club Queen

FAN-FAVOURITE PERFORMANCE:
"Fancy" by Iggy Azalea vs. Reba McEntire

What's the T?

A seasoned artist serving equally high glam and edgy androgynous looks, Phoenix (Brian Trapp) from Atlanta is also the drag daughter of the legendary Nicole Paige Brooks. In the 10 years of drag before appearing on the third season of *Drag Race*, Phoenix not only showcased her production and dance ability on stages across the South but she is a formidable costume designer, inspired by pop culture and designers like Alexander McQueen and Thierry Mugler. Though only lasting two episodes in her season, losing a Lady Gaga "Bad Romance" lip sync challenge to Delta Work following the "Queens in Space" challenge, Phoenix used her experience on *Drag Race* to continue the evolution of her persona, changing her aesthetic and elevating her artistry to the high standard she presents today. With a strong sense of community in mind, Phoenix continues to perform across the South and now works as one of the top nightclub entertainment directors in Atlanta.

DRAG TERM

Okurr

Originating in a comedy web series about
character Shocantelle Brown then popularised by
Laganja Estranja, "okurr" is a way of saying "okay"
adding sass with a rolling r. "It's very dry, it's almost
kinda like your vagina. Okurr!" – Laganja Estranja

DRAG TERM

Reading

An advanced format of the insult, "reading" is the art of criticising by wittily and incisively exposing a person's flaws (i.e. "to read them like a book"). On *RuPaul's Drag Race*, queens are invited to participate in "The Library" (referring to the act of one reading a book in a library), a mini challenge in where contestants read their fellow queens "to filth" (to thoroughly insult them, or to call attention to flaws).

Porkchop

"Victoria is very outgoing ... she likes to meet men..."

Quick Stats

DRAG RACE:
Season 1

RANKING:
9th place

POST DRAG RACE:
Featured as part of the Miley Cyrus performance of "Dooo It!" at the 2015 MTV Video Music Awards; continues entertaining crowds with the *Dreamgirls Revue* alongside *Drag Race* alumni Shannel and Morgan McMichaels; featured in an episode of *RuPaul Drives*

SIGNATURE LOOK:
Miss America Pageant Realness

TYPE:
The Old School Showgirl

FAN-FAVOURITE PERFORMANCE:
"A Song for You/When We Were Young/I'm Here Medley" by The Carpenters, Adele and Jennifer Hudson

What's the T?

Beginning her drag career in 1987, Victoria "Porkchop" Parker was created from the mind of North Carolina's Victor Bowling. An astute and well-seasoned pageant queen, Porkchop has participated in over 200 pageants, won over 100 and taken four national titles including Miss Continental Plus in 2003. Inspired by Elizabeth Taylor, Porkchop's aesthetic is classic pageant drag, which has served her well for over two decades. Porkchop has starred in two documentaries on the pageantry system: *Trantasia* (2006) a documentary on The World's Most Beautiful Transexual Pageant and *Pageant* (2008) as a lead cast member vying for the title of Miss Gay America.

Cast in the first season of *RuPaul's Drag Race*, Porkchop holds the title of the first queen eliminated from the entire show, and as a result receives a warm welcome from RuPaul herself at all of the live reunion shows. Although an already polished and expert drag performer, it was Porkchop's weak sewing skills that brought about her early dismissal in the first challenge. Porkchop gave a show-stopping performance of RuPaul's "Supermodel" against Akashia in the first ever Lip Sync for Your Life of the series.

Porkchop has relentlessly toured since Season 1 concluded in 2009 and was lucky enough to be featured on stage with over 30 other drag queens at the 2015 MTV Video Music Awards for the Miley Cyrus performance. As part of RuPaul's DragCon 2018 Porkchop competed in the first ever Miss DragCon Pageant and came out on top, snatching the title from the likes of other first eliminated queens such as Naysha Lopez and Tempest DuJour.

The Princess

"Putting on the makeup, the wig, the costume... unleashes her!"

Quick Stats

DRAG RACE:
Season 4

RANKING:
11th place

SIGNATURE LOOK:
Andro Eclecticism Realness

TYPE:
The Punk Princess

FAN-FAVOURITE PERFORMANCE:
"Welcome to the Black Parade" by My Chemical Romance

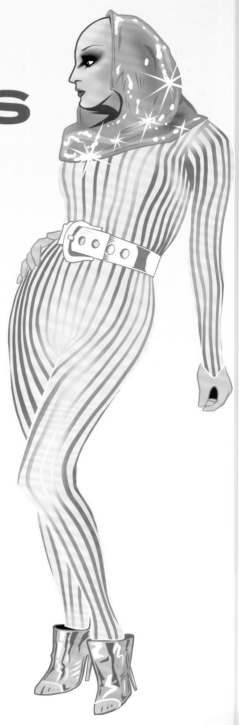

What's the T?

A queen who isn't afraid of flipping a wig and serving bald beauty is Chicago's The Princess (Adam Biga), who delivers a mash-up of avant garde and couture, eclectic and posh drag. Born in Johannesburg, South Africa, and self taught in makeup, styling and dressmaking since the age of 18, The Princess's first ever audition saw her cast in Season 4 where she found herself among other edgy and atypical queens like Sharon Needles. However, after two low performances in the "Glamazons vs. Champions" commercial and "WTF!: Wrestling's Trashiest Fighters" challenges and two lip syncs for her life, The Princess was eliminated much earlier in the competition than was expected for a queen with her experience. Evolving her aesthetic to challenge the boundaries of drag, The Princess continues to serve up looks for days on her Instagram, performs regularly in Nashville and has been a fan-favourite at RuPaul's DragCon in recent years.

THE
CESS

Raja

"I have a Master's degree in Fierce... I should be a professor!"

Quick Stats

DRAG RACE:
Season 3

RANKING:
Winner

POST DRAG RACE:
Toured the US as Iggy Azalea's principal makeup artist; co-host of World of Wonder's *Fashion Photo RuView* with Raven; released singles "Diamond Crowned Queen" (2011),"Zubi Zubi Zubi" (2013) and "Cholita" (2015); toured her one-woman shows Gawdess (2017) and Masque (2018)

SIGNATURE LOOK:
Around The World In 80 Days Realness

TYPE:
The Drag Chameleon

FAN-FAVOURITE PERFORMANCE:
"In My Arms" by Kylie Minogue

What's the T?

LA's Sutan Amrull has performed as Raja Gemini for over 20 years as a self-described "glitter hippie, artist, performer, model and muse". Having dropped out of university, Raja decided early on that she had a flair for the artistic – painting, drawing and makeup artistry. Raja started drag in the early 1990s house music club scene where she created thrift store outfits and joined other punk club queens in the LA night life. Inspired by Leigh Bowery and rebelling against the sequins and shoulder pads, the edgy Raja was born and began not only her drag career but started working as a makeup artist. This artistry has formed the basis of Raja's career, which has seen her not only tour with Adam Lambert as his principal makeup artist, but saw her serve as makeup artist for nine cycles of Tyra Banks' *America's Next Top Model*.

Competing in *RuPaul's Drag Race* was a walk in the park for the likes of Raja – a seasoned performer with incomparable wit and sewing skills. Winning three main challenges and stealing the scene at every runway in looks ranging from African Zulu Realness to Rainbow Brite Cosplay, Raja easily took the crown, beating fellow "Heather" Manila Luzon and Alexis Mateo in the final episode.

In the years following her win, Raja has released her own offbeat and edgy music videos and singles including the Latino pop "Cholita" (2015) and Bollywood electro-disco "Zubi Zubi Zubi" (2013). Raja also now stars in the weekly web series *Fashion Photo RuView* with Raven, with whom she was also a Drag Professor on the spin-off show *RuPaul's Drag U.*

RAJA

Raven

"I'm a man in a dress – I'm a psychological woman."

Quick Stats

DRAG RACES:
Season 2 | *All Stars* 1

RANKING:
2nd place | 2nd place

POST DRAG RACE:
Co-host of World of Wonder's *Fashion Photo RuView*; music video pin-up (MNDR's "Feed Me Diamonds"); star of *RuPaul's Drag Race* spin-offs *Drag U* and *Drag My Dinner Party* with Jujubee and Manila Luzon

SIGNATURE LOOK:
Dark Temptress Realness

TYPE:
The Stone Cold Vixen

FAN-FAVOURITE PERFORMANCE:
"Megacolon" by Fischerspooner

What's the T?

After a stint as a male go-go dancer by the name of Phoenix, David Petruschin from Riverside, California took flight and and emerged as Raven in the West Hollywood drag scene in 2002. Raven started her drag career alongside legendary sisters Morgan McMichaels and Mayhem Miller, performing shows that suited her taste for the underground – stylish and electronic. A fan of non-mainstream artists like Fischerspooner, Róisín Murphy and Miss Kittin, Raven's performance style separated her from the pack as a dark horse.

Raven appeared on the second season of *RuPaul's Drag Race* and soon became a fan-favourite for her quick wit, icy yet fierce composure and striking aesthetic. Raven's style was equally matched with her makeup artistry, which saw her execute so many varied looks from baby blue blushing bride to Cabaret-era Liza, and country sweetheart realness to disco-diva-meets-accomplished-author. Although incredibly determined and styled to the gods, Raven was pipped at the post by both Tyra Sanchez in Season 2 and Chad Michaels in the first season of *All Stars*.

Following the *Race*, Raven co-hosted the weekly web series *Fashion Photo RuView* with Season 3 winner Raja, summoning her expert style, hair and makeup knowledge to "toot and boot" the looks of new *Drag Race* contestants on the runway. Commencing with Season 9 of *Drag Race*, Raven was appointed as a Creative Producer and makeup artist for RuPaul herself, beating the mug of mother for the gawds, earning her a fierce Emmy nomination in 2018 for her work on the show.

Rebecca Glasscock

"If I'm so horrible and such a bitch, why would I give you my brand new green contacts?"

Quick Stats

DRAG RACE:
Season 1

RANKING:
3rd place

SIGNATURE LOOK:
High School Sweetheart Realness

TYPE:
The Original Fish

FAN-FAVOURITE PERFORMANCE:
"Show Me How You Burlesque"
by Christina Aguilera

What's the T?

Fort Lauderdale's Rebecca Glasscock (Javier Rivera), who found her drag surname in a gay men's dating magazine, appeared on Season 1 after performing for several years in her local bar scene under the guidance of drag mother Misty Eyez. The OG fish, Rebecca made her entrance into the werkroom serving girl-next-door realness contrasting with some of the more outlandish and body-revealing looks presented by her castmates. A favourite of the judges for her realness, a reserved Rebecca often found herself in hot water with her fellow contestants who would cite the favouritism when it came to Rebecca's makeover main challenge win and subsequent top three placing. While not often performing alongside her *Race* sisters outside of reunion gigs, Glasscock has continued to perform and has pursued an acting career, successfully landing a cameo as an alien drag queen in *Men in Black 3*.

Robbie Turner

"Am I the first girl that has ever broken a light on the runway?"

Quick Stats

DRAG RACE:
Season 8

RANKING:
7th place

SIGNATURE LOOK:
Vintage Vixen Realness

TYPE:
The Classic Cinema Queen

FAN-FAVOURITE PERFORMANCE:
"The Name Game" by Jessica Lange
from *American Horror Story*

What's the T?

After a one-off stint as a Liza Minnelli in 2005, Seattle's Robbie Turner (Jeremy Baird) caught the drag bug and began her career as a full-time performer impersonating the likes of Lady Gaga and Kylie Minogue before morphing into the old-Hollywood queen audiences saw on Season 8. Ready to serve impressive period looks that channel the starlets of 1930s–60s cinema, Robbie entered the *Race* with big shoes to fill as previous Seattle contestants Jinkx Monsoon and BenDeLaCreme revealed how important being well-read on history and artistry is to drag performers from that city. Although Robbie found herself on roller skates lip syncing for her life early in the contest, she channelled her inner Deborah Harry in the "New Wave Queens" challenge, taking the win in front of Debbie herself! While she has a keen eye for period fashion, it was her costume construction skills in the "Wizards of Drag" challenge that cut Robbie's time on *Drag Race* short. Since then, Turner has focused her time into writing *I'll Tell You for Free*, a book and solo show that tells the "tales, follies and inconceivable truths from the life of a drag queen".

Roxxxy Andrews

"I'm Roxxxy Andrews and I'm here to make it clear..."

Quick Stats

DRAG RACES:
Season 5 | *All Stars* 2

RANKING:
Co-runner Up | 4th place

POST DRAG RACE:
Toured as Tamar Braxton's principal makeup artist; competed in 2015 Miss Gay Southernmost USofA Pageant (1st Runner Up); featured on RuPaul's single "Read U Wrote U" (2016)

SIGNATURE LOOK:
Pageant Perfection Realness

TYPE:
The Thick 'N' Juicy Queen

FAN–FAVOURITE PERFORMANCE:
"Talent Medley (at Miss Gay Southernmost USofA 2015)" by Various Artists

What's the T?

At 21 Michael Feliciano from Orlando made his first appearance in drag at a Halloween celebration and soon became the pageant beauty Roxxxy Andrews. Her namesake a fusion of *Chicago*'s Roxie Hart and her drag mother, the legendary Erica Andrews, Roxxxy was inspired by the Orlando drag pageant scene. Drag sister of Detox, who also hails from Orlando, Roxxxy had taken numerous pageantry titles in her formative years including Miss West Virginia Continental Plus 2008 and 2009, the prestigious Miss Continental Plus 2010 and Miss West Virginia Continental 2012. In 2013 Roxxxy Andrews was cast in *RuPaul's Drag Race* alongside drag sisters Detox and Alaska with whom the clique "Rolaskatox" was formed. A formidable contestant throughout, Roxxxy won the first costuming challenge as well as the "Super Troopers" makeover challenge. In an iconic Lip Sync for Your Life performance Roxxxy executed a wig reveal to Willow Smith's "Whip My Hair" that floored judges RuPaul and Michelle Visage who admitted, "I think I peed a little bit. Serious!". Finishing as a co-runner up with fan-favourite Alaska, Roxxxy Andrews fought heavy criticism from the public for her perceived bullying of winner Jinkx Monsoon.

Following *Drag Race* Roxxxy took on the role as principal makeup artist for Tamar Braxton (whom she impersonated in the "Snatch Game") on her US tour and walked the Marco Marco runway in 2014. Returning to serve sickening looks on the *All Stars* 2 runway, Roxxxy Andrews' journey to fourth place may have been the result of "Rolaskatox" voting strategies but she managed to "Ru-deem" herself with audiences with a new humble attitude towards the competition.

Realness

"Realness" can be used to describe the act of appearing feminine, but the term can also follow a noun to describe the act of appearing to be a convincing realistic, authentic, or accurate version of said noun. For example: "BeBe Zahara Benet was serving jungle queen realness!", meaning BeBe's presentation was amazing; I believed she was truly a queen of the jungle.

DRAG TERM

Serve

To present oneself in a particular way to the best of your ability and, in the context of drag performance, giving the audience what they want. Inspired by a queen's runway presentation you could say something like: "Detox was serving some *Fifth Element* realness on the runway last night – she gave me life!".

Sahara Davenport

"Competition is on bitches!"

Quick Stats

DRAG RACE:
Season 2

RANKING:
7th place

SIGNATURE LOOK:
Runway Fish Realness

TYPE:
The Ballet School Beauty Queen

FAN-FAVOURITE PERFORMANCE:
"Medley" by Whitney Houston

What's the T?

A queen from NYC who always aimed to entertain the kids, school the girls and spread fierceness throughout the land, Sahara Davenport (Antoine Ashley) was not only a shining star of the city's drag scene but was also the partner of *Drag Race* sister Manila Luzon. While living in Dallas as a college student, Sahara started her career utilising her classical training in dance to get a foothold in the world of drag artistry before being cast in Season 2 in 2010. Winner of the "Starrbootylicious" challenge demonstrating her charisma, uniqueness, nerve and talent with a stripper pole, Sahara went on to pirouette her way through a lip sync contest against Morgan McMichaels and rock it out in the "Rocker Chicks" challenges before being eliminated. After the *Race*, Sahara was one of the first ever Racers to release her own dance singles ("Go Off" and "Pump with Me" are bonafide pop jams)! Sadly, in 2012 Sahara Davenport passed away from heart failure. Her legacy lies in the humility of her persona and her fierce attitude, which will be remembered by *Drag Race* fans for years to come as the series' "eternal queen".

Sasha Belle

"I feel like I have cracked the code."

Quick Stats

DRAG RACE:
Season 7

RANKING:
13th place

SIGNATURE LOOK:
Gun-slingin' Glam Realness

TYPE:
The Drag Mom of Iowa

FAN-FAVOURITE PERFORMANCE:
"Crazy in Love (2014 Remix)"
by Beyoncé

What's the T?

A former Miss Gay Iowa who presides over her own hometown drag contest series for newcomers, Sasha Belle (Jared Breakenridge) is a young drag mother that got her start in 2006. A self-proclaimed *Drag Race* scholar and mega fan, Sasha's sixth audition for the *Race* was her golden ticket into the cast of Season 7 where she brought her mash-up of camp glamour and club-ready chameleon to the cut. After a not-quite-nude illusion in the first week's challenge, Sasha found herself among the bottom queens before being eliminated the following week after a forgettable performance in the "Glamazonian Airways" challenge and an unrealised "jet set eleganza" runway presentation. While her time on *Drag Race* didn't live up to Sasha Belle's expectations, she has continued to value her time on the show while directing and producing *Sasha Belle's Drag Race* back home in Iowa.

Sasha Velour

"Gender is a construct – tear it apart!"

Quick Stats

DRAG RACE:
Season 9

RANKING:
Winner

SIGNATURE LOOK:
Graphic Brow Realness

TYPE:
The Wearable Art Queen

FAN-FAVOURITE PERFORMANCE:
"This Woman's Work" by Kate Bush

What's the T?

Inspired by gender expression, visual artistry and queer history, it was through study abroad in Russia that Sasha Velour (Sasha Steinberg) built on what had been a lifetime of playing with dress-up to curate a drag persona and aesthetic that encapsulates the spirit of icons such as Leigh Bowery and Grace Jones. Sasha's trademark bald head is not only a tribute to her late mother who battled cancer, but speaks to her desire to challenge generic drag clichés and craft a new definition for drag beauty. Entering the Season 9 werkroom with a scream, Sasha delivered high fashion, high colour and intelligent takes on the challenges each week, with two maxi challenge wins alongside Shea Couleé in the "Good Morning Bitches!" and TV pilot challenges. A true runway panther, Sasha Velour delivered epic eleganza, with her "Gayest Ball Ever" creations and makeover looks pushing her through to the finale where, after two theatre-shaking Whitney Houston lip sync battles, she won the ninth *Drag Race* crown. In what has become the year of Sasha Velour, she not only took the title of America's Next Drag Superstar, but was awarded Drag Queen of the Year as well as Best Visual Artist at the 5th Annual Brooklyn Nightlife Awards in 2017.

Since her win, Sasha continues to produce her monthly drag epic Nightgowns in New York City, has released her own *Drag Race* look book and directed her own drag magazine *Velour*, while her artistry has featured in *Vogue*, *Vanity Fair* and *Cosmopolitan*. Sasha Velour's Cosmo Queens transformation video alone has racked up more than 7.5 million views – now that's nothing to joke about!

Serena ChaCha

"This is the best quinceañera present ever!"

Quick Stats

DRAG RACE:
Season 5

RANKING:
13th place

SIGNATURE LOOK:
Miss Panama Realness

TYPE:
The Educated Queen

**FAN-FAVOURITE
PERFORMANCE:**
"Grown Woman" by Beyoncé

What's the T?

A fine arts student from Panama with a keen interest in surrealism as well as soft sculpture and its relationship with the artistry of drag, Serena ChaCha (Myron Morgan) built her drag persona for three years before her appearance on Season 5 of *Drag Race*. Serving super-sweet-sixteen realness on her arrival in the werkroom, the sweetness turned sour with her castmates backstage in the Untucked lounge after a poor performance in the "Lip Sync Eleganza Extravaganza" and some sideways comments about how her education plays a role in her drag artistry. In one of the most famous scenes of Untucked, Serena found herself ambushed by almost the entire cast of Season 5 after calling other queens "ghetto" and "uneducated" before a lip sync against Monica Beverly Hillz to Rihanna's "Only Girl". While her time on the *Race* was short and explosive, Serena ChaCha's career following the show has focused on elevating her brand of Latina glamazon drag while building her own custom wig empire as both a stylist and savvy businesswoman!

Shangela

"Halleloo!"

Quick Stats

DRAG RACES:
Season 2 | Season 3 | *All Stars* 3

RANKING:
12th place | 6th place | 3rd/4th place

POST DRAG RACE:
Starred on *Dance Moms* in 2011 as a guest mentor teaching her signature Death Drop; teamed up with Lady Gaga and Courtney Act in the lyric video of Gaga's "Applause"; released dance singles "Werqin' Girl" (2012) and "Pay Me" (2018); appeared in the movie *A Star Is Born* (2018)

SIGNATURE LOOK:
Post-modern-pimp-ho Realness

TYPE:
The Sickening Southern Belle

FAN-FAVOURITE PERFORMANCE:
"Turn Me Out" by Praxis ft. Kathy Brown

What's the T?

A comedian from Paris, Texas, DJ Pierce – better known as Shangela Laquifa Wadley – started performing drag professionally in 2009. She was only five months into her career in the LA drag scene before being cast in the second season of *RuPaul's Drag Race*. A member of the Haus of Edwards, Shangela cites *Drag Race* alumni Alyssa Edwards as her drag mother. Although being eliminated first in Season 2 and subsequently winning the Entertainer of the Year 2010 pageant in Los Angeles, Shangela was re-cast in the third season of *Drag Race* where she finished in sixth place after a strong performance throughout the season. Shining in her characterisation of "Laquifa – the post-modern-pimp-ho" in the "Ru Ha Ha" comedy challenge, it was evident that while sewing wasn't necessarily her strong point, Shangela is one hell of a performer. The character of Laquifa went on to star on stage in her own comedy show as well as on *One Night Stand Up* on Logo TV.

A fan-favourite *Drag Race* moment, Shangela's "out of the box" appearance in Season 3 was spoofed in Season 4 when Shangela announced she was cast in that competition. A "werqin' girl" through and through, Shangela has continued to deliver stand-up comedy sets, including the Bianca Del Rio Roast for her 40th birthday.

Appearing in the third season of *All Stars* as the first queen ever to compete in three separate seasons of *Drag Race*, Shangela delivered killer comedic performances in the "Divas Lip Sync Live", "Snatch Game" and "My Best Squirrelfriend's Dragsmaids Wedding Trip" challenges. Despite being a front runner for the crown, Shangela was pipped at the post by Trixie and Kennedy who were chosen by the eliminated queens to advance to the finale. In her time since the *Race*, Shangela has not only been a busy queen on the small screen with appearances in TV shows *Dance Moms*, *Glee* and *2 Broke Girls*, but she starred alongside Willam in the Bradley Cooper/Lady Gaga led *A Star Is Born* in 2018.

Shannel

"I am amazed at myself... "

Quick Stats

DRAG RACES:
Season 1 | *All Stars* 1

RANKING:
4th place | 3rd/4th place

SIGNATURE LOOK:
39 Character Illusions Realness

TYPE:
The Original Body Queen

**FAN-FAVOURITE
PERFORMANCE**:
"My Immortal" by Evanescence

What's the T?

A drag legend with roots in both Las Vegas and California, more than two decades of mastery in the art of female impersonation and the first body queen of *Drag Race*, Shannel (Bryan Watkins) is a diva for all seasons. An unparalleled (ex-Chanel) makeup artist with the ability to transform into countless different characters, Shannel appeared on the first season of *Drag Race* with not only the body but the charisma, uniqueness, nerve and talent to take out the crown. While Shannel's confidence often came off as her playing the grande dame, her aesthetic execution was always impeccable and her devotion to her artistry never wavered. Her iconic Medusa lip sync to Whitney Houston's "The Greatest Love of All" and the "I am beautiful" moment before the judges, bolstered her status as a legendary queen of the *Race*. She was soon cast in the first season of *All Stars*, where she won three main challenges in a row with Chad Michaels. Following her time on Season 1, Shannel appeared as a professor on *Drag U*, as well as working on hair and makeup behind the scenes. In recent years, she has moved back to Las Vegas where she is one of the most in-demand queens on The Strip.

NNEL

Sharon Needles

"Happy Halloween everybody!"

Quick Stats

DRAG RACE:
Season 4

RANKING:
Winner

POST DRAG RACE:
Released singles "I Wish I Were Amanda Lepore" (2014), "Dracula" (2015) and "666" (2018); spokesperson for People for the Ethical Treatment of Animals (PETA); was honoured by the Pittsburgh City Council declaring 12 June 2012 the official "Sharon Needles Day"

SIGNATURE LOOK:
Undead Goth Gurl Realness

TYPE:
The B-movie Beauty

FAN-FAVOURITE PERFORMANCE:
"Sweet Transvestite" from *The Rocky Horror Picture Show (Original Soundtrack)*

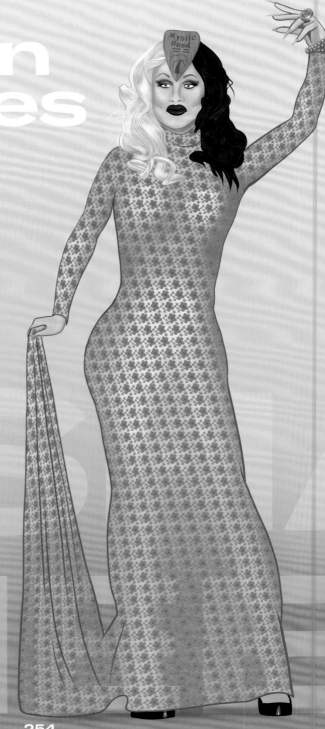

What's the T?

Originally from Iowa, Sharon Needles moved to Pittsburgh in 2004 where she began working as a drag performer in nightclubs and later with the legendary experimental troupe the Haus of Haunt, which Needles described as "one punk rock, messy mash up of very talented, fucked up weirdos". It was here that Aaron Coady became the legendary Sharon Needles of today. The Pittsburgh collective included fellow *Drag Race* alumni, and later partner, Alaska, who shone through the season after Needles' debut.

In 2012 Needles appeared on the fourth season of *Drag Race* and quickly gained a dedicated fan base dying for her ghoulish, original style – in a season heavy with fishy, fashion-focused queens. Less an underdog than someone completely ignored among the breastplates and sparkles, Needles repeatedly performed well – winning four of the challenges and only having to lip sync for her life once (where she battled it out with on-screen nemesis Phi Phi O'Hara). In the close-run finale, Needles snatched the crown from Chad Michaels to become The Next Drag Superstar.

Since *Drag Race*, Needles has busied herself releasing albums *PG-13* (2013), *Taxidermy* (2015) and *Battle Axe* (2017). Sharon Needles has also become the face of PETA and has hosted horror and suspense B-movies on Logo TV. Sharon continues to tour her solo material across the world and snatched wigs alongside legends Lady Bunny, Lypsinka and Varla Jean Merman at the 2018 Wigstock revival on Pier 17 in New York City.

DRAG TERM

Sickening

To be beyond awesome, incredibly amazing, or particularly attractive in appearance or performance. Alexis Mateo from Season 3 famously told us that being a drag queen in the United States was not only "BAM!" but that she is "Sickening! No?".

DRAG TERM

Squirrel friends

A term used to describe a girlfriend who, just like a
squirrel, hides her nuts.

Shea Couleé

"I didn't come to play,
I came to slay."

Quick Stats

DRAG RACE:
Season 9

RANKING:
3rd/4th place

SIGNATURE LOOK:
Leotarded Lemonade Realness

TYPE:
The Boujie Banjee Queen

**FAN-FAVOURITE
PERFORMANCE:**
"Partition" by Beyoncé

What's the T?

A queen with a background in costume design and a doctorate in FIERCE, Chicago's Shea Couleé (Jaren Merrell) has served equal parts boujee and bourgie since her 2012 start in local drag competition Roscoe's Drag Race. Following in the footsteps of her fellow windy city sisters Pearl and Kim Chi, Shea appeared on Season 9 of *Drag Race* entering the werkroom, furry armed and leotarded, determined to nab the crown. Stealing the show as Blac Chyna in the musical challenge, snatching back-to-back team wins with Sasha Velour in the pilot and talk show challenges and then gloriously taking home the win for the "Gayest Ball Ever", Shea Couleé executed one of the best runs in *Drag Race* herstory all the while stomping the runway like a pro ("why y'all acting brand new?"). In one of the season's biggest shocks, Shea found herself lip syncing for the crown against new sister Sasha, to Whitney Houston's "So Emotional" and was ultimately pipped at the post. Determined to slay regardless, Shea Couleé's debut EP *Couleé-D* and its music video anthology dropped as Season 9 wound up to a close, giving fans a healthy dose of Beyoncé's Lemonade teas with a fierce serve of Couleé brilliance. Following her time on the *Race*, Shea has toured her new material around the world – including singles "Crème Brûlée" and "Gasoline" – and chronicled her journeys in web series *Call Me Couleé*.

SHEA COULEÉ

Sonique

"My mom sent me to a military school in hopes that she'd get a little soldier. Needless to say she got a drag queen!"

Quick Stats

DRAG RACE:
Season 2

RANKING:
9th place

SIGNATURE LOOK:
Buxom Bombshell Realness

TYPE:
The Backflip Belle of the South

FAN-FAVOURITE PERFORMANCE:
"Love Hangover/Heartbreaker" by Mariah Carey

What's the T?

A small-town showgirl who worked the Atlanta scene alongside local legends Angelica D'Paige and Shawnna Brooks, Sonique (Kylie Sonique Love) began her drag career at landmark club Blake's on the Park. Sauntering into Season 2, this Georgia peach brought her Southern charm and backflips to the main stage as she fought for the crown before a gutting post-"Snatch Game" elimination against new friend Morgan McMichaels. Sonique revealed in the reunion that she had been in the process of transitioning, which was held off during the audition and filming of the show. In living her truth after her season, the ever-fierce Sonique moved to LA, has walked the runway with Marco Marco and continues entertaining week-in-week-out on the Southern California scene as part of showcasts at Micky's and the *Dreamgirls Revue*.

Stacy Layne Matthews

"Henny!"

Quick Stats

DRAG RACE:
Season 3

RANKING:
8th place

SIGNATURE LOOK:
Curvy Country Glam Realness

TYPE:
The Back Swamp Beauty Queen

**FAN-FAVOURITE
PERFORMANCE:**
"Diamonds (Live)" by Rihanna

What's the T?

The undisputed breakout star of Season 3, Stacy Layne Matthews – or Queen Henny as her fans have dubbed her – from Back Swamp, North Carolina, had been performing in drag and participating in pageants for almost nine years before being cast in Season 3 of *Drag Race*. A small-town queen with the biggest heart of her season, Stacy (Stacy Jones) entered the *Race* with skills as a theatre buff and gifted singer, with her acting chops nabbing her a win in the "Snatch Game" as Mo'Nique. Unfortunately, it was Stacy's seamstress abilities that saw her serve a not-so-sweet red velvet cake couture creation in the "Face, Face, Face of Cakes" challenge which landed her in RuPaul's firing line. Since the *Race*, Stacy continues to perform in drag, has produced her first NYC cabaret show From Stacy, With Love..., featured in the AAA GIrls' 2017 single "Heather", and in 2019 guest starred in the fourth season of *All Stars* with her very own themed challenge – "Super Girl Groups, Henny".

Tammie Brown

"I don't see you out there walking children in nature."

Quick Stats

DRAG RACES:
Season 1 | *All Stars* 1

RANKING:
8th place | 9th/10th place

POST DRAG RACE:
Released albums *Popcorn* (2009), *Discos Undead* (2010) and *Hot Skunx* (2014); member of the band Rollz Royces with *Drag Race* alumni Kelly Mantle and long-time collaborator Michael Catti; starred in an advertisement for travel company Orbitz with fellow *All Stars* alumni Raven, Manila Luzon and Latrice Royale

SIGNATURE LOOK:
Yesteryear Glam Realness

TYPE:
The Countess of Kooky

FAN-FAVOURITE PERFORMANCE:
"What's Love Got to Do with It" by Tina Turner

What's the T?

A drag icon of the Southern California scene, Tammie Brown – the creation of Keith Glen Schubert – got her start doing drag as a teenager in theatre productions of *Grease* and *Into the Woods*. Inspired by Tina Turner as well as Dustin Hoffman's *Tootsie*, Brown delivers an original blend of drag that recalls old Hollywood with an eccentric twist. Prior to her appearance on *Drag Race*, Tammie appeared on *The Surreal Life* and *How Clean Is Your House?*, and auditioned unsuccessfully for *America's Got Talent*.

Joining the first cast of *RuPaul's Drag Race*, Tammie was already one to stand out from the pack of nine queens vying for the title of the first America's Next Drag Superstar. Although her appearance lasted two episodes, Tammie – in true Brown fashion – vowed not to lip sync for her life to Michelle Williams' "We Break the Dawn" against Akashia and simply smiled and danced back and forth into elimination. An iconic appearance at the Season 1 reunion saw Brown go head to head with RuPaul and the judges on the merits of her drag and bullying from the judges – neither Ru nor Tammie were having a bar of it! The all-round zaniness of Tammie Brown won her a spot in the first season of *All Stars* where we were all "teleported to Mars".

After her *Drag Race* stints, Tammie Brown has continued to release offbeat folk and pop music including singles "Whatever", "Clam Happy", "Love Piñata" and "Walking Children in Nature" with Michael Catti. On the social justice front, our #QueenWithACause has continued her famous educational nature walks with city youth and has advocated to Free the Orcas from Seaworld in the United States. Tammie Brown's inspirational imagination just hasn't stopped, as she has begun selling her own unique handmade dolls – Rag Queenz – online and at RuPaul's DragCon.

Tatianna

"Thank you."

Quick Stats

DRAG RACES:
Season 2 | *All Stars* 2

RANKING:
4th place | 6th place (originally 8th)

SIGNATURE LOOK:
Teen Queen Superstar Realness

TYPE:
The Femme Fatale

**FAN-FAVOURITE
PERFORMANCE:**
"The Same Parts" by Tatianna

266

What's the T?

A queen who had started playing with drag as early as 14 years old, Tatianna (Joey Santolini) entered Season 2 having only performed in drag a handful of times. Often judged by the other queens in her season as inexperienced, relying on her looks or simply being a judge's favourite, Tatianna fought tooth and nail to prove that she deserved to compete for the title of America's Next Drag Superstar, winning the "Snatch Game" as Britney Spears and delivering consistent performances in the main challenges. It was Tatianna's fierceness in the face of dismissive competitors and immense growth after the show that led to her casting in the second season of *All Stars*, where the beauty queen of Virginia was given a chance to prove her star quality to a modern *Drag Race* audience. Slaying the talent show with her spoken word performance "The Same Parts", audiences saw Tati turning it out week after week, culminating in an epic Rihanna lip sync against Alyssa Edwards demanding a double "shantay you stay". A bonafide fan-favourite, Tatianna has toured worldwide, release singles from her debut record *T1* – "Try" and "CYA"– in 2018, hosted her own web series *T With Tati* and rocked the MTV Video Music Awards red carpet in full Aaliyah impersonation drag!

Tempest DuJour

"Who's ready for some hot tuna casserole? 'Cause mama's home."

Quick Stats

DRAG RACE:
Season 7

RANKING:
14th place

SIGNATURE LOOK:
Colourful Campy Realness

TYPE:
The Drag Professor

FAN-FAVOURITE PERFORMANCE:
"Defying Gravity" from *Wicked*

What's the T?

Arizona university professor Tempest DuJour (Patrick Holt) had only started doing drag 10 years before appearing on the seventh season of *Drag Race*, citing a love for Shakespearean theatre and camp aesthetics. Having been one of the go-to stock photography queens for years, the immediately recognisable face of drag, Mama Tempest (she's got two!) appeared on *Drag Race* popping out her own offspring in a hilarious werkroom entrance. After a heated squabble about being an older queen with competitor Kandy Ho, this delicate flower of the desert found herself lip syncing to RuPaul's "Geronimo" against Kandy after a crabby nude illusion runway presentation. Eliminated first from her cut of queens, Tempest DuJour has been described as one of the strongest "first out" from the entire series and has continued entertaining fans in her WOWPresents featured videos, her starring role in the 2017 drag queen comedy film *Cherry Pop* and turned the Miss DragCon pageant on its head with a Patti Page-come-Cardi B performance nabbing her a tie for runner up with Season 8's first out, Naysha Lopez.

Thorgy Thor

"Aww. Jesus. Gross."

Quick Stats

DRAG RACES:
Season 8 | *All Stars 3*

RANKING:
6th place | 10th place

SIGNATURE LOOK:
Fashion Clown Realness

TYPE:
The Dreadlocks Darling

**FAN-FAVOURITE
PERFORMANCE:**
"Philip Seymour Hoffman"
by Thorgy Thor

What's the T?

An alternative drag performance artist who got her start performing drag characters in theatre shows, Thorgy Thor (Shane Thor Galligan) worked the New York and Brooklyn scenes for over 12 years prior to appearing on *Drag Race* – including winning the LEGEND Award at the 2014 Brooklyn Nightlife Awards. An accomplished violinist inspired by NYC icon Joey Arias, Thorgy auditioned for every season of *Drag Race* before Ru decided that Thorgy had relaxed and was ready for Season 8. A consistently safe queen in the challenges, Thorgy delivered colourfully chic runway presentations that were complemented by her superbly smart performances in the "Snatch Game" as Michael Jackson and in her writing of the "Street Meatz" New Wave parody. The unfortunate victim of Chi Chi DeVayne's drag assassination in the "Black and White" runway lip sync to "And I Am Telling You I'm Not Going", Thorgy left the competition far earlier than many fans had hoped.

Looking good and feeling Thorgeous, Thorgy returned to the *Race* in *All Stars* 3 ready to shake the bad Bob spirits from Season 8 to showcase her unique zany take on drag. Despite a solid violin act in the "All Star Variety Show", Thorgy found herself eliminated following Divas Lip Sync Live as her Stevie Nicks failed to conjure the magic that her competitors did with their impersonations. Following her time on *Drag Race*, Thorgy has ensured her local NYC fans receive their regular dose of her Thorgeousness, while her longtime dream orchestra show Thorgy's Thorchestra finally saw fruition in 2018.

The T

The T, also spelled Tea or Tee, refers to the "truth" in terms of gossip, news, information or true facts – "What's the t?" ("What's up?"). Often predicating or following a commentary or a "read" are the phrases "No tea, no shade" (i.e. "I don't mean to disrespect you"), or "All tea, all shade" (meaning: "I don't care if this offends you"). For example: "No tea, no shade – but plastic surgery wouldn't be the worst thing to happen to you".

Throwing shade

The act of subtly and wittily insulting someone; an underhand comment or backhanded compliment; bitchiness personified. Throwing shade is something the drag community have been doing for years, and so have you – you just didn't know it had a name. Here's some shade you might like to throw: "You're so confident. I just love how you don't even care what you look like."

Trinity K. Bonet

"The 'K' is for Kardashian but we don't use that for legal reasons."

Quick Stats

DRAG RACE:
Season 6

RANKING:
7th place

SIGNATURE LOOK:
Sasha Fierce Realness

TYPE:
The Young Glamazon

**FAN-FAVOURITE
PERFORMANCE:**
"Formation" by Beyoncé

What's the T?

A pageant queen with an exceptionally supportive stage mother to keep her showgirl in check, Trinity K. Bonet (Joshua Jones) is another queen who had her start in drag after a Halloween performance at a family party. Inspired to make her ill mother proud by auditioning, Trinity took her expansive drag collection into Season 6 with her eyes on the prize and a sense of old-school drag skill and performance that represented her roots in both Miami and Atlanta. Straight out of the gate, Trinity demonstrated masterful costume construction and makeup artistry with her party supplies inspired Queen Amidala meets geisha look, which continued throughout the *Race* with more show-stopping costumes. It was Trinity's initial closed-off nature that bore the brunt of castmate Bianca Del Rio's criticism. However, after an empowering sharing of her HIV story and a personal breakthrough with her own competition goals, Trinity soared and won over the judges and fans alike. Eliminated after a stumble in the "Drag Queens of Talk" interview challenge, Trinity has focused her energy after *Drag Race* into curating her impeccable Beyoncé impersonation act and snatching pageant crowns including Miss Sweetheart International 2015.

Trinity the Tuck

"I call shade!"

Quick Stats

DRAG RACES:
Season 9 | *All Stars* 4

RANKING:
3rd/4th place | Winner

SIGNATURE LOOK:
Silicone Siren Realness

TYPE:
The Master Mother Tucker

**FAN-FAVOURITE
PERFORMANCE:**
"Titanium/Bionic" by David Guetta/Sia
& Christina Aguilera

What's the T?

The bad-ass beauty with a Kardashian booty, Trinity "The Tuck" Taylor (Ryan Taylor) is an Alabama-born queen who got her start in Orlando, Florida. An entertainer who effortlessly teeters the lines of high glamour and working girl, Trinity is the ultimate pageant queen who not only has the drag girl parody down – check out La'Whore's "Shlong" – but was crowned with the highest pageant honour of Entertainer of the Year in 2014, beating out *Drag Race* alum Alyssa Edwards (who placed runner up). Easily the queen to beat from the outset, Trinity delivered a *Drag Race* run that was not only full of straight-up gag for her inimitable tuck, but demonstrated growth while she had audiences laughing all the way to the finale with her shelarious winning performances in the "9021-HO" and "Draggily Ever After" challenges. Having turned out ass-out iconic Taylor looks all season – and even snatching a win for her makeover of crew member Rizzo – Trinity's final four presentation was a pageant fan's dream, while her lip sync performance against Peppermint, although not successful, kept audiences cheering on the Trin Train.

Since her time on Season 9 Trinity has not only toured the world but has produced her own look book, starred in makeup tutorials for her own channel and for *Cosmopolitan*, produced shelarious videos starring her iconic Sister Mary Kuntz character and has even created her own video game app *Stanky's Big Adventure*! When the cast of *All Stars* 4 was announced, fans the world across were tightening their tucks in anticipation of Trinity's return to win the biggest pageant crown of all. Slaying the entire competition taking home four wins (worth $20,000 dawlahs!) and turning out some of the most exquisite runway presentations the show has ever seen, Trinity proved to audiences that she had what it takes to be the next member of the All Stars Hall of Fame alongside Monét X Change. A queen with one of the highest amount of wins ever for a contestant, Trinity The Tuck has bolstered her status as a fan-favourite who is now not only an Entertainer of the Year, but a world class legend of the *Race*.

Trixie Mattel

"I'm like the knock-knock joke of drag."

Quick Stats

DRAG RACES:
Season 7 | *All Stars* 3

RANKING:
6th place (originally 11th) | Winner

POST DRAG RACE:
Guest starred on *American Horror Story: Roanoke* as herself; starred in Viceland series *The Trixie & Katya Show* alongside Season 7 sister Katya; released her own makeup collection called Oh Honey!, with Sugarpill in 2018

SIGNATURE LOOK:
Life-in-plastic Realness

TYPE:
The Life-size Doll

FAN-FAVOURITE PERFORMANCE:
"Moving Parts" by Trixie Mattel

What's the T?

Brian Firkus of Milwaukee, Wisconsin, began his drag career as Trixie Mattel, rebelling against the abusive relationship he had with his stepfather, reclaiming the name "Trixie" that her stepfather used as a slur. Though she won her first and only pageant in Milwaukee, Trixie was cut from a different yarn to many pageant queens, so a move to Chicago made for a fresh career challenge. It was here that she began working with Chicago club icon Kim Chi and perfected her now legendary overdrawn Barbie-inspired mug and curated the comedic drag act fans across the world have grown to love.

Cast in Season 7 of *Drag Race*, Trixie Mattel was an instant favourite for not only her original look but for her quick wit. Although shining in the "Glamazonian Airways" challenge, Trixie soon faced criticism for not standing out from the pack in her team's parody "Tan With U" and lost her Lip Sync for Your Life against Pearl. Following heavy criticism on social media for eliminating Trixie, RuPaul brought back all of the eliminated contestants in the "Conjoined Queens" challenge to earn a spot back in the competition for another two weeks. A clear fan-favourite from the outset, Trixie Mattel was cast in the third season of *All Stars* where her bombshell wigs and comedy stylings reached new heights, snatching top positions in the "My Best Squirrelfriend's Dragsmaids Wedding Trip" and "Pop Art Ball" challenges, which helped push her into the final two alongside Kennedy Davenport, where she ultimately snatched the crown and entered the Drag Race Hall of Fame alongside Chad Michaels and Alaska.

Mattel's star continues to rise along with her fanbase numbers as a result of not only her viral YouTube series (*UNHhhh*)-turned-Viceland television series (*The Trixie & Katya Show*), but her debut country/folk records *Two Birds* and *One Stone* – the former reaching #5 on the UK Country charts and the latter reaching #1 on the US Heatseekers (new artist) charts. With hit tracks under her belt and now over 1.5 million followers on Instagram awaiting her next moves, Trixie Mattel's brand of plastic fantastic fantasy has truly taken over!

Tyra
Sanchez

"I'm not a bitch – I'm America's sweetheart."

Quick Stats

DRAG RACE:
Season 2

RANKING:
Winner

POST DRAG RACE:
Became the subject of documentary film *Drag Dad* about her role as both a drag queen and father; starred as a fierce Drag Professor on *RuPaul's Drag U*; appeared as a Kim Zolciak doppelgänger on an episode of *The Real Housewives of Atlanta*

SIGNATURE LOOK:
Red Carpet Beyoncé Realness

TYPE:
The Seasoned Ingénue

FAN-FAVOURITE PERFORMANCE:
"Drunk in Love" by Beyoncé

What's the T?

Florida's James Ross IV began his drag career after leaving high school at age 16. Raised by her drag mother who brought her out of homelessness, Tyra Sanchez was taught the trade of old-school Florida pageant drag and began impersonating Beyoncé in shows across the Orlando gay scene. Looking to challenge herself and bring about a new life for her young son, Jeremiah, Tyra was cast in the second season of *RuPaul's Drag Race*. Despite her youth, Tyra demonstrated a wide array of drag tricks and sickening stage looks. Winning three main challenges, Sanchez brought out her comedic side in the "Country Queens" challenge and was complimented by RuPaul for her old-school drag conduct in the "Here Comes the Bride" runway. Tyra's off-stage bridezilla drama with Tatianna provided iconic Untucked moments bringing the supplementary show to the forefront in its early inception. Never having to lip sync for her life, Tyra Sanchez took the crown in a photo finish against Raven in a performance of RuPaul's "Jealous of My Boogie".

The youngest contestant to ever take the title of America's Next Drag Superstar, Tyra Sanchez went on to release her first single "Look at Me" in 2011 and work on a Kickstarter-funded feature documentary by Björn Flóki called *Drag Dad*. Since winning the crown, Tyra (who now goes by the moniker Tyra 007) has taken a step back from the *Drag Race* spotlight, which she revealed in a 2015 episode of web series *Hey Qween* was the result of her focusing on being the caretaker parent for her son Jeremiah in the formative years of his schooling.

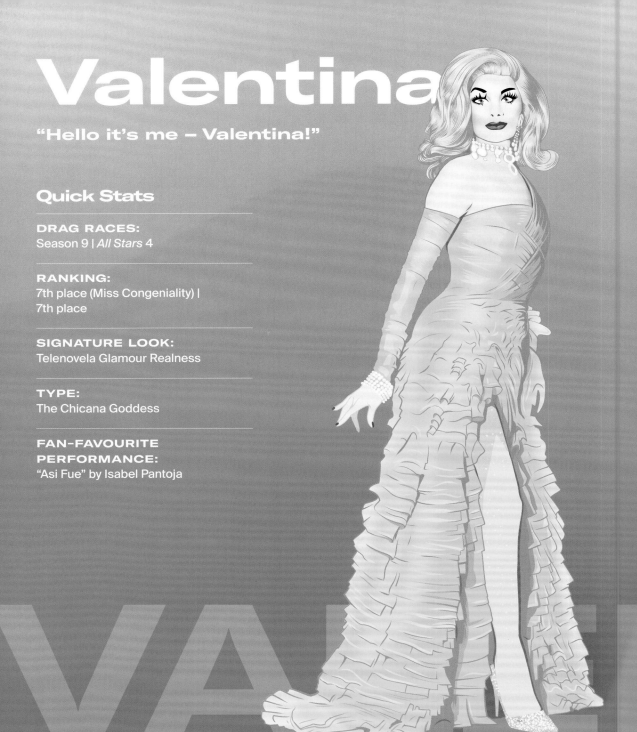

Valentina

"Hello it's me – Valentina!"

Quick Stats

DRAG RACES:
Season 9 | *All Stars* 4

RANKING:
7th place (Miss Congeniality) |
7th place

SIGNATURE LOOK:
Telenovela Glamour Realness

TYPE:
The Chicana Goddess

**FAN-FAVOURITE
PERFORMANCE:**
"Asi Fue" by Isabel Pantoja

What's the T?

A young queen with a refreshing take on classic drag performance and style, Valentina (James Leyva) famously performed live in drag venues for only 10 months before appearing on the ninth season of *Drag Race*. A well researched queen of unparalleled beauty and poise, Valentina served not only looks that complemented her Mexican heritage but she also brought humility and kindness to the show with the aim of showing that a Latin queen doesn't need to be the butt of jokes, but a role model. After a stumble in the TV pilot challenge with Nina Bo'Nina Brown, Valentina found herself eliminated in the first ever Lip Sync for Your Life where RuPaul stopped the contest, demanding Valentina take an obstructing mask away from her mouth. Valentina admitted that while the competition got the better of her and she wasn't prepared for the lip sync, she is ready to show the world that the fierceness she demonstrated up until that point will help propel her career as the future face of Latin American drag.

In the years after her first appearance on *Drag Race* Valentina became a household name as she has graced the pages of *Vogue México*, appeared in makeup tutorials for *Vogue*'s YouTube channel, featured in *America's Next Top Model* alongside Katya and Manila Luzon, and starred in her very own web series *La Vida De Valentina*. Ready to "Rudeem" herself and prove her talent to the world, Valentina entered *All Stars* 4 with a new found sense of confidence... and desire to fulfil her French vanilla fantasy! Slaying the "Super Girl Groups, Henny" challenge as Selena and tearing the main stage to shreds in a lip sync performance to Ariana Grande's "Into You", Valentina proved that she is a formidable lip sync performer and dancer. While early in the competition Valentina soared, she found herself eliminated by friend Latrice Royale after a not-so-chic "Club 96" creation in the "Queens of Club" challenge. Going on to star in Fox's televised production *Rent: Live* in 2019, Valentina shows no sign of her All Star beauty fading, and fans worldwide are eager to see what their diva with a heart has in store for them next!

Vanessa Vanjie Mateo

"Miss Vanjie... Miss Vanjie... Miss... Vanjie..."

Quick Stats

DRAG RACE:
Season 10

RANKING:
14th place

SIGNATURE LOOK:
Eloquent Ghetto Hooker Realness

TYPE:
The Banjee Babe

**FAN–FAVOURITE
PERFORMANCE:**
"Miss DragCon Medley" by Various

What's the T?

Originally hired as a backing dancer for drag mother (and *Drag Race* All Star) Alexis Mateo, Vanessa Vanjie Mateo (Jose Cancel) soon found herself competing in local pageants and performing in the local Tampa drag scene in Florida. Getting her life (or should we say getting these cookies!) as a fierce young competitor on the 10th season of *Drag Race*, Miss Vanjie came onto screens as a firecracker in the personality department. While her on-screen persona was serving fierce and her drag serving fish, her costuming floundered in the "Drag on a Dime" first challenge and Vanjie found herself lip syncing against Kalorie Karbdashian-Williams straight off the bat in front of Christina Aguilera herself!

Eliminated far too soon, it was Vanessa Mateo's backwards exit that caused an internet sensation, which was not only a gay mating call, but the greatest meme of 2018. Truly a first-out to be remembered, Miss Vanjie – who has already graced the cover of *Gay Times* – broke the internet and found her catchphrase uttered throughout Season 10 by her sisters and enabled her to tour the world showcasing the potential talent we missed on season on our screens. Will we see more of Miss Vanjie? Only time will tell...

Venus D-Lite

"I don't think you can be the Next Drag Superstar with no confidence."

Quick Stats

DRAG RACE:
Season 3

RANKING:
13th place

SIGNATURE LOOK:
"Who's That Girl" Realness

TYPE:
The Iconic Impersonator

FAN-FAVOURITE PERFORMANCE:
"Dress You Up" by Madonna

What's the T?

With the title of being the only male Madonna impersonator in a major motion picture – *The Comebacks* (2007) – Los Angeles' Venus D-Lite (Adam Guerra) is one of the world's premier impersonators of the Queen of Pop and has enjoyed a successful full-time career as a drag queen since studying at film school. A regular on the West Hollywood scene like many Racers from Season 3 of *Drag Race*, Venus was only able to entertain audiences with her brash yet colourful persona for one episode after a blunder in the "Queens Who Mopped Xmas" costume challenge, which resulted in a wig-flipping messy lip sync against Shangela. Since appearing on *Drag Race*, Venus D-Lite has not only kept her Madonna impersonation act at the top of booking agents' charts, but she has appeared on the reality shows *My Strange Addiction* and *Botched*. Venus can also be found in the *Ripley's Believe It or Not Annual*, which cites her expensive obsession with emulating the Material Girl – racking up more than $175,000 in plastic surgery costs!

Tuck

The act of a drag queen pulling back his genitals
using duct tape or tight underwear to create the
illusion of having a flat and feminine crotch area.
A "meaty tuck" (as described by RuPaul about
Season 1's Jade) is a poorly executed tuck, which
is large, lumpy or bulging.

DRAG TERM

Werk

To do something with a large amount of fiery attitude, vitality and vigour with the intent to impress and stun. "Werk" can also be used as an exclamation of approval: "You better werk bitch!" – RuPaul.

Violet Chachki

"Pain is beauty and I'm the prettiest."

Quick Stats

DRAG RACE:
Season 7

RANKING:
Winner

POST DRAG RACE:
Released debut EP *Gagged* (2015) featuring single "Bettie" starring Pearl in the music video; performs "The Night Before Christmas" on the Christmas album *Christmas Queens* (2015); became the first drag queen to model for a major lingerie ad campaign with Bettie Page Lingerie

SIGNATURE LOOK:
Von Teese Pin-up Realness

TYPE:
The Burlesque Bondage Beauty

FAN-FAVOURITE PERFORMANCE:
"Million Dollar Man" by Lana Del Rey

What's the T?

Starting her career using a fake ID to gain entry into local Atlanta drag shows, Violet Chachki (Jason Dardo) was taken under the wing of drag mother Dax ExclamationPoint (who later appeared on Season 8 of *Drag Race*) and soon became a regular cast member at nightclub Jungle. Working alongside Amanda Lepore and drag royalty Lady Bunny, Violet quickly cut her teeth and learned not only how to beat her face for the gods but learned burlesque show tricks like waist cinching and aerial silk performance. Chachki came into early notoriety for being photographed in possession of Sharon Needles' official winner's crown after it was stolen during a 2012 gig in Atlanta – Chachki was later found innocent of the theft.

In 2015 Chachki was cast in *Drag Race*, serving week after week of unmatchable runway looks. Winning the first main challenge, despite criticism from Michelle Visage for her un-cinched "boy body", Violet Chachki went on to win three main costume-based challenges. An expert in design and costume execution, her "I really could die bitch" 18-inch waist runway presentation floored the judges and fellow competitors. Chachki never fell into the bottom two and took the crown from Ginger Minj and Pearl in the live taped reunion finale. Much like young winner Tyra Sanchez, Chachki received heavy criticism for her cold and bitchy yet determined performance throughout the season.

Following her win on *Drag Race* Chachki has released her debut EP *Gagged*, attended the 2015 MTV Video Music Awards as Miley Cyrus' red carpet partner (and performed onstage with her that year too!), walked for Moschino's Fall 2018 collection at Milan Fashion Week and has taken her aerial burlesque talents to the next level, touring in Dita Von Teese's The Art of the Teese.

Vivacious

"Mother has arrived!"

Quick Stats

DRAG RACE:
Season 6

RANKING:
12th place

SIGNATURE LOOK:
90s Club-Kid Realness

TYPE:
The Legendary Neon Queen

**FAN-FAVOURITE
PERFORMANCE:**
"Twisted" by Peter Rauhofer

What's the T?

Vivacious (Osmond Vacious) – one of the original 1990s NYC club-kids –
has spent more than two decades creating an intergalactic drag explosion
of colour, futurism and pop art as a performer and DJ. Having worked
predominantly in the straight nightclub scene in New York, Vivacious' "living
art" aims to bridge the gap between the gay and straight communities – her
appearance on Season 6 providing her an opportunity to school the children
across the world.

Entering the werkroom stalled by a zipper malfunction revealing a lit-up
glittered head named Ornacia, Vivacious' offbeat character and quotable
catchphrases won over audiences immediately, even though her costume
construction and "Scream Queens" acting efforts didn't inspire the judges.
After two lip syncs against Kelly Mantle and April Carrión, Vivacious and
Ornacia were sent on their way back to NYC leaving a newer understanding
of yesteryear's club-kid style, which inspired its own runway challenge in
Season 9. Since appearing on *Drag Race* Vivacious has appeared in several
WOWPresents webisodes, performed on MTV with Miley Cyrus and joined
Katy Perry on stage on *Saturday Night Live* in 2017 vogueing and cracking her
fans, keeping the club-kid vibe alive!

Vivienne Pinay

"I will always be the fishiest queen today, tomorrow, next month, the past seasons, and the next seasons to come."

Quick Stats

DRAG RACE:
Season 5

RANKING:
10th/11th place

SIGNATURE LOOK:
Goddess Glam Realness

TYPE:
The Fierce Filipina Fish

FAN-FAVOURITE PERFORMANCE:
"Minaj Medley" by Nicki Minaj

What's the T?

Having created her drag persona watching *RuPaul's Drag Race* since its inception, New York's Vivienne Pinay (Michael Donehoo) had been working in the beauty industry for almost a decade before competing for the crown in Season 5. A goddess with Filipino heritage and an unclockable Nicki Minaj impersonation act, Vivi came, slayed and conquered as far as her runway presentations and makeup transformations were concerned. After a lacklustre lip sync to Britney Spears' "Oops I Did It Again", Vivienne and Honey Mahogany found themselves ousted in the first-ever double elimination of the series. Maintaining a friendship with Alyssa Edwards after Season 5, Pinay not only worked on-set as a personal assistant and makeup artist on the *Alyssa's Secret* web series, but she was made an honorary member of the House of Edwards, appearing in her own spin-offs of the series impersonating her new drag mother.

The Vixen

"I'm just here to fight!"

Quick Stats

DRAG RACE:
Season 10

RANKING:
7th place

SIGNATURE LOOK:
Black Girl Magic Realness

TYPE:
The Fiery Queen

FAN-FAVOURITE PERFORMANCE:
"Endangered Species/Angry Black Woman" by Dianne Reeves & Porsha O

What's the T?

Hailing from the South Side of Chicago, The Vixen (Anthony Taylor) started her drag career in 2013 inspired by her love for 1920s vintage style and determined to intertwine social justice and activism in her performance style. Having built a career on her outspoken viewpoint on race relations and a fierce drag talent, The Vixen was able to create a unique drag concert – *Black Girl Magic* – in 2016, which has toured across the United States showcasing the best and brightest queens of colour. Following the footsteps of Chicago sisters DiDa Ritz and Shea Couleé (with whom she'd featured on the single "Cocky" in 2017), The Vixen appeared on the 10th season of *RuPaul's Drag Race* ready to take the crown... by any means necessary! While her personality appeared to clash on screen with the likes of Eureka, it became clear that The Vixen was ready to educate and bring to light the unfair treatment of queens of colour in the context of the show, while snatching the win for the "PharmaRusical" challenge. After three killer lip syncs for her life, The Vixen was finally eliminated after a stumble in the "Unauthorized Rusical" challenge. Not ready to back down – even after a heated clash with RuPaul in the Season 10 reunion – The Vixen continues to bring her passionate brand of drag to stages across the States while speaking out on race issues that encircle drag, *Drag Race* and the wider gay community.

Willam

"I'm not gonna RuPaulogize for anything that I'm doing now."

Quick Stats

DRAG RACE:
Season 4

RANKING:
7th place

POST DRAG RACE:
Performed as a member of viral drag troupe DWV as well as with the AAA Girls; released solo albums *The Wreckoning* (2012) and *Shartistry In Motion* (2015); starred in TV's *The New Normal* (2013) and *CSI* (2012) and the film *Kicking Zombie Ass for Jesus* (2015); produces YouTube series *Beatdown* and *Paint Me Bitch*

SIGNATURE LOOK:
Whore Clown Realness

TYPE:
The Model, Actress, Mattress, Whorespondent, Ice Cream Man

FAN-FAVOURITE PERFORMANCE:
"Rich Girl" by Hall and Oates

What's the T?

Willam Belli's drag career began somewhat simultaneously with her acting career in the early 2000s with appearances on *The District*, *Boston Public* and her starring role on *Nip/Tuck* as transgender woman Cherry Peck. Supplementing her acting career with live performance, Willam formed the band Tranzkuntinental with fellow drag queens Detox, Vicky Vox, Kelly Mantle and Rhea Litré in 2009 before releasing her own solo parody "The Vagina Song" in 2012. Cast in the fourth season of *RuPaul's Drag Race*, Willam was from the outset an accomplished screen queen with killer comedy chops to boot – a rule-breaker with impeccable style. Never forgetting to name-drop a co-star, designer shoe or ex *Sex and the City*-worn Dolce and Gabbana coat, Willam presented realness on the main stage and slayed the competition winning the "Float Your Boat" main challenge. Although a fan-favourite, Willam's time on *Drag Race* was short lived after a series of rules were broken in the now famous "What Did Willam Do?" shock elimination.

Willam can be credited as one of the hardest working *Drag Race* alumni with the release of two full-length solo albums and over 20 singles (including her girl group foray with Alaska and Courtney Act as the AAA Girls), her shelarious web content like *Beatdown*, *Paint Me Bitch* and *¿Cómo Se Dice?*, which has garnerned more than 180 million views on her YouTube channel, as well as her first ever book – *Suck Less: Where There's a Willam There's a Way* – paving the glitter-smudged pathway for queens to follow for years to come. Continuing to demonstrate that she is a successful drag queen who doesn't have to show for a dollar, Willam also starred alongside Shangela in the Lady Gaga/Bradley Cooper smash *A Star Is Born* in 2018.

Yara Sofia

"Echa pa'lante."

Quick Stats

DRAG RACES:
Season 3 | *All Stars* 1

RANKING:
4th place (Miss Congeniality) |
5th/6th place

SIGNATURE LOOK:
Gothic Latina Realness

TYPE:
The Dark-Sided Queen

**FAN-FAVOURITE
PERFORMANCE:**
"Work Your Body/Echa Pa'Lante"
by Thalia

What's the T?

Commanding the arts of makeup, costume design, hair manipulation and, of course, drag, Puerto Rico's Yara Sofia (Gabriel Burgos Ortiz) was inspired by the dark Finnish-American actress Maila Nurmi and the designs of Alexander McQueen to create a persona that was equally sweet and evil. One of the standouts of Season 3 of *RuPaul's Drag Race*, Yara Sofia took gothic drag to the mainstream with countless original presentations on the main stage, earning her the respect of queens for her uniqueness and talent but also the public, who crowned her Miss Congeniality of the season. Her unparalleled hair artistry gave her a main challenge win, which led to her casting in the first season of *All Stars* – where she brought her classic Latina charm and humour to win the "RuPaul's Gaff-In" challenge with Team Yarlexis partner Alexis Mateo. In the years after her appearance on *All Stars*, Yara has walked Marco Marco runways, performed across the world and has moved to Las Vegas where she is now one of the key queens on The Strip, bringing her brand of hyper-glam-Latina-goth-fantasy to the fans of Sin City.

Yuhua Hamasaki

"Can you feel the shade?"

Quick Stats

DRAG RACE:
Season 10

RANKING:
12th place

SIGNATURE LOOK:
Ankh You Glad To See Me Couture

TYPE:
The Sickening Seamstress

**FAN-FAVOURITE
PERFORMANCE:**
"Miley Medley" by Miley Cyrus

What's the T?

Chinese-born New Yorker Yuhua Hamasaki (Yuhua Ou) started playing with dressing up as a teen, inspired by the crazy creatives she saw on MySpace, and would find her tribe on the LGBTQ scene as a 16-year-old drag queen. After almost 10 years of entertaining, designing the queens of the city's costumes and appearing on TV shows such as *Big Ang* and *Saturday Night Live*, Yuhua landed on the 10th season of *Drag Race* ready to snatch the crown. Despite having made an impression with her bubbly personality, it was her failure to land a joke in the "Tap That App" challenge and her poorly executed feathers runway eleganza that ousted her from the competition. While her time on the *Race* was short, Yuhua's reunion look inspired by *The Ring* gave audiences one last gag at this queen's ability to mix style and comedy. Although she didn't snatch the crown, Yuhua – who won the pageant title of Miss Fire Island (2012) – continues to tour her hot and flexible body across the United States while dishing up some brilliant reads on her Twitter!

LIPS

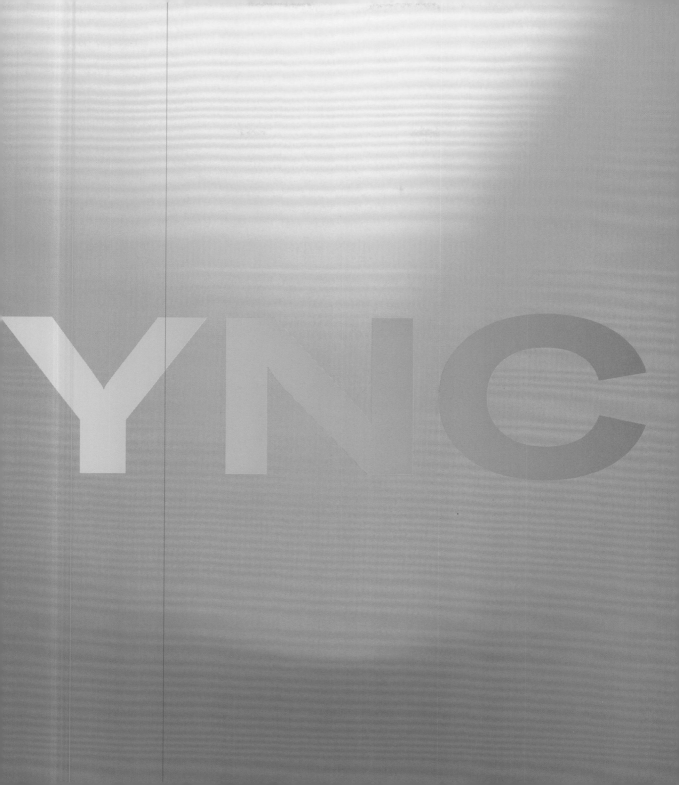

Season 1

EP	CONTESTANTS	SONG	ELIMINATED
1	Akashia vs. Victoria "Porkchop" Parker	"Supermodel (You Better Work)" By RuPaul	Victoria "Porkchop" Parker
2	Akashia vs. Tammie Brown	"We Break the Dawn" By Michelle Williams	Tammie Brown
3	Akashia vs. Shannel	"The Greatest Love of All" By Whitney Houston	Akashia
4	Jade vs. Rebecca Glasscock	"Would I Lie to You" By Eurythmics	Jade
5	BeBe Zahara Benet vs. Ongina	"Stronger" By Britney Spears	Ongina
6	Rebecca Glasscock vs. Shannel	"Shackles" By Mary Mary	Shannel
8	BeBe Zahara Benet vs. Nina Flowers	"Cover Girl (Put the Bass in Your Walk)" By RuPaul	Nina Flowers

Season 2

EP	CONTESTANTS	SONG	ELIMINATED
1	Sahara Davenport vs. Shangela	"Cover Girl (Put the Bass in Your Walk)" By RuPaul	Shangela
2	Nicole Paige Brooks vs. Raven	"My Lovin' (You're Never Gonna Get It)" By En Vogue	Nicole Paige Brooks
3	Mystique Summers Madison vs. Raven	"I Hear You Knockin" By Wynonna Judd	Mystique Summers Madison
4	Morgan McMichaels vs. Sonique	"Two of Hearts" By Stacey Q	Sonique
5	Morgan McMichaels vs. Sahara Davenport	"Carry On" By Martha Wash	Morgan McMichaels
6	Jujubee vs. Sahara Davenport	"Black Velvet" By Alannah Myles	Sahara Davenport
7	Jessica Wild vs. Tatianna	"He's the Greatest Dancer" By Sister Sledge	Jessica Wild
8	Jujubee vs. Pandora Boxx	"Shake Your Love" By Debbie Gibson	Pandora Boxx
9	Jujubee vs. Tatianna	"Something He Can Feel" By Aretha Franklin	Tatianna
11	Raven vs. Tyra Sanchez	"Jealous of My Boogie" By RuPaul	Raven

Season 3

EP	CONTESTANTS	SONG	ELIMINATED
2	Venus D-Lite vs. Shangela	"The Right Stuff" By Vanessa Williams	Venus D-Lite
3	Delta Work vs. Phoenix	"Bad Romance" By Lady Gaga	Phoenix
4	India Ferrah vs. Mimi Imfurst	"Don't Leave Me This Way" By Thelma Houston	Mimi Imfurst
5	India Ferrah vs. Stacy Layne Matthews	"Meeting in the Ladies Room" By Klymaxx	India Ferrah
6	Delta Work vs. Mariah	"Looking for a New Love" By Jody Watley	Mariah
7	Alexis Mateo vs. Stacy Layne Matthews	"Knock On Wood" By Amii Stewart	Stacy Layne Matthews
8	Delta Work vs. Manila Luzon	"MacArthur Park" By Donna Summer	Delta Work
9	Carmen Carrera vs. Yara Sofia	"Mickey" (Spanish Version) By Toni Basil	No Elimination
10	Carmen Carrera vs. Shangela	"Believe" By Cher	Carmen Carrera
11	Alexis Mateo vs. Shangela	"Even Angels" By Fantasia	Shangela
12	Carmen Carrera vs. Raja	"Straight Up" By Paula Abdul	Carmen Carrera
13	Alexis Mateo vs. Yara Sofia	"I Think About You" By Patti LaBelle	Yara Sofia
15	Manila Luzon vs. Raja	"Champion" By RuPaul	Manila Luzon

Season 4

EP	CONTESTANTS	SONG	ELIMINATED
1	Alisa Summers vs. Jiggly Caliente	"Toxic" By Britney Spears	Alisa Summers
2	Lashauwn Beyond vs. The Princess	"Bad Girls" By Donna Summer	Lashauwn Beyond
3	DiDa Ritz vs. The Princess	"This Will Be (An Everlasting Love)" By Natalie Cole	The Princess
4	Madame LaQueer vs. Milan	"Trouble" By Pink	Madame LaQueer
5	Kenya Michaels vs. Milan	"Vogue" By Madonna	Kenya Michaels
6	Jiggly Caliente vs. Milan	"Born This Way" By Lady Gaga	Milan
7	Jiggly Caliente vs. Willam	"Mi Vida Loca (My Crazy Life)" By Pam Tillis	Jiggly Caliente
8	Phi Phi O'Hara vs. Sharon Needles	"It's Raining Men (The Sequel)" By Martha Wash and RuPaul	No Elimination; (Willam Disqualified)
9	DiDa Ritz vs. Latrice Royale	"I've Got to Use My Imagination" By Gladys Knight	DiDa Ritz
10	Kenya Michaels vs. Latrice Royale	"(You Make Me Feel Like) A Natural Woman" By Aretha Franklin	Kenya Michaels
11	Chad Michaels vs. Latrice Royale	"No One Else on Earth" By Wynonna Judd	Latrice Royale
13	Chad Michaels vs. Phi Phi O'Hara vs. Sharon Needles	"Glamazon" By RuPaul	No Elimination

Season 5

EP	CONTESTANTS	SONG	ELIMINATED
1	Penny Tration vs. Serena ChaCha	'Party in The U.S.A." By Miley Cyrus	Penny Tration
2	Monica Beverly Hillz vs Serena ChaCha	"Only Girl (in the World)" By Rihanna	Serena ChaCha
3	Coco Montrese vs. Monica Beverly Hillz	"When I Grow Up" By The Pussycat Dolls	Monica Beverly Hillz
4	Honey Mahogany vs. Vivienne Pinay	"Oops!... I Did It Again" By Britney Spears	Honey Mahogany & Vivienne Pinay (Double Elimination)
5	Detox vs. Lineysha Sparx	"Take Me Home" By Cher	Lineysha Sparx
6	Coco Montrese vs. Jade Jolie	"I'm So Excited" By The Pointer Sisters	Jade Jolie
7	Alyssa Edwards vs. Roxxxy Andrews	"Whip My Hair" By Willow Smith	No Elimination
8	Alyssa Edwards vs. Ivy Winters	"Ain't Nothin' Goin' on But the Rent" By Gwen Guthrie	Ivy Winters
9	Alyssa Edwards vs. Coco Montrese	"Cold Hearted" By Paula Abdul	Alyssa Edwards
10	Coco Montrese vs. Detox	"(It Takes) Two to Make it Right" By Seduction	Coco Montrese
11	Detox vs. Jinkx Monsoon	"Malambo No. 1" By Yma Sumac	Detox
12	Alaska vs. Jinkx Monsoon vs. Roxxxy Andrews	"The Beginning" By RuPaul	No Elimination

Season 6

EP	CONTESTANTS	SONG	ELIMINATED
1	Kelly Mantle vs. Vivacious	"Express Yourself" By Madonna	Kelly Mantle
2	Darienne Lake vs. Magnolia Crawford	"Turn the Beat Around" By Vicki Sue Robinson	Magnolia Crawford
3	April Carrión vs. Vivacious	"Shake It Up" By Selena Gomez	Vivacious
4	April Carrión vs. Trinity K. Bonet	"I'm Every Woman" By Chaka Khan	April Carrión
5	Gia Gunn vs. Laganja Estranja	"Head to Toe" By Lisa Lisa & Cult Jam	Gia Gunn
6	Milk vs. Trinity K. Bonet	"Whatta Man" By Salt-N-Pepa with En Vogue	Milk
7	BenDeLaCreme vs. Darienne Lake	"Point of No Return" By Exposé	No Elimination
8	Joslyn Fox vs. Laganja Estranja	"Stupid Girls" By Pink	Laganja Estranja
9	Adore Delano vs. Trinity K. Bonet	"Vibeology" By Paula Abdul	Trinity K. Bonet
10	Adore Delano vs. Joslyn Fox	"Think" By Aretha Franklin	Joslyn Fox
11	BenDeLaCreme vs. Darienne Lake	"Stronger (What Doesn't Kill You)" By Kelly Clarkson	BenDeLaCreme
12	Adore Delano vs. Bianca Del Rio vs. Courtney Act vs. Darienne Lake	"Sissy That Walk" By RuPaul	Darienne Lake

Season 7

EP	CONTESTANTS	SONG	ELIMINATED
1	Kandy Ho vs. Tempest DuJour	"Geronimo" By RuPaul	Tempest DuJour
2	Katya vs. Sasha Belle	"Twist of Fate" By Olivia Newton-John	Sasha Belle
3	Jasmine Masters vs. Kennedy Davenport	"I Was Gonna Cancel" By Kylie Minogue	Jasmine Masters
4	Pearl vs. Trixie Mattel	"Dreaming" By Blondie	Trixie Mattel
5	Kandy Ho vs. Mrs. Kasha Davis	"Lovergirl" By Teena Marie	Mrs. Kasha Davis
6	Jaidynn Diore Fierce vs. Kandy Ho	"Break Free" By Ariana Grande	Kandy Ho
7	Jaidynn Diore Fierce vs. Max	"No More Lies" By Michel'le	Max
8	Ginger Minj vs. Sasha Belle vs. Jaidynn Diore Fierce vs. Tempest DuJour	"I Think We're Alone Now" By Tiffany	Jaidynn Diore Fierce
9	Miss Fame vs. Pearl	"Really Don't Care" By Demi Lovato	Miss Fame
10	Ginger Minj vs. Trixie Mattel	"Show Me Love" By Robin S	Trixie Mattel
11	Katya vs. Kennedy Davenport	"Roar" By Katy Perry	Katya
12	Ginger Minj vs. Kennedy Davenport vs. Pearl vs. Violet Chachki	"Born Naked" By RuPaul	Kennedy Davenport

Season 8

EP	CONTESTANTS	SONG	ELIMINATED
1	Laila McQueen vs. Naysha Lopez	"Applause" By Lady Gaga	Naysha Lopez
2	Dax ExclamationPoint vs. Laila McQueen	"I Will Survive" By Gloria Gaynor	Dax ExclamationPoint & Laila McQueen (Double Elimination)
3	Cynthia Lee Fontaine vs. Robbie Turner	"Mesmerized (Freemasons Radio Edit)" By Faith Evans	Cynthia Lee Fontaine
4	Chi Chi DeVayne vs. Naysha Lopez	"Call Me" By Blondie	Naysha Lopez
5	Acid Betty vs. Naomi Smalls	"Causing a Commotion" By Madonna	Acid Betty
6	Derrick Barry vs. Robbie Turner	"I Love It" By Icona Pop ft. Charli XCX	Robbie Turner
7	Chi Chi DeVayne vs. Thorgy Thor	"And I Am Telling You I'm Not Going" from *Dreamgirls*	Thorgy Thor
8	Bob the Drag Queen vs. Derrick Barry	"You Make Me Feel (Mighty Real)" By Sylvester	Derrick Barry
9	Bob the Drag Queen vs. Chi Chi DeVayne vs. Kim Chi vs. Naomi Smalls	"The Realness" By RuPaul	Chi Chi DeVayne

Season 9

EP	CONTESTANTS	SONG	ELIMINATED
2	Jaymes Mansfield vs. Kimora Blac	"Love Shack" By The B-52's	Jaymes Mansfield
3	Aja vs. Kimora Blac	"Holding Out for a Hero" By Bonnie Tyler	Kimora Blac
4	Charlie Hides vs. Trinity Taylor	"I Wanna Go" By Britney Spears	Charlie Hides
5	Cynthia Lee Fontaine vs. Farrah Moan	"Woman Up" By Meghan Trainor	No Elimination (Eureka Removed Due to Injury)
6	Cynthia Lee Fontaine vs. Peppermint	"Music" By Madonna	Cynthia Lee Fontaine
7	Aja vs. Nina Bo'Nina Brown	"Finally" By CeCe Peniston	Aja
8	Alexis Michelle vs. Farrah Moan	"Baby I'm Burnin" By Dolly Parton	Farrah Moan
9	Nina Bo'Nina Brown vs. Valentina	"Greedy" By Ariana Grande	Valentina
10	Nina Bo'Nina Brown vs. Shea Couleé	"Cool for the Summer" By Demi Lovato	Nina Bo'Nina Brown
11	Alexis Michelle vs. Peppermint	"Macho Man" By The Village People	Alexis Michelle
12	Peppermint vs. Sasha Velour vs. Shea Couleé vs. Trinity Taylor	"U Wear It Well" By RuPaul	No Elimination
14 A	Peppermint vs. Trinity Taylor	"Stronger" By Britney Spears	Trinity Taylor
14 B	Sasha Velour vs. Shea Couleé	"So Emotional" By Whitney Houston	Shea Couleé
14 C	Peppermint vs. Sasha Velour	"It's Not Right, But It's Okay" By Whitney Houston	Peppermint

Season 10

EP	CONTESTANTS	SONG	ELIMINATED
1	Kalorie Karbdashian-Williams vs. Vanessa Vanjie Mateo	"Ain't No Other Man" By Christina Aguilera	Vanessa Vanjie Mateo
2	Eureka vs. Kalorie Karbdashian-Williams	"Best of My Love" By The Emotions	Kalorie Karbdashian-Williams
3	Mayhem Miller vs. Yuhua Hamasaki	"Celebrity Skin" By Hole	Yuhua Hamasaki
4	Dusty Ray Bottoms vs. Monét X Change	"Pound the Alarm" By Nicki Minaj	Dusty Ray Bottoms
5	Mayhem Miller vs. Monét X Change	"Man! I Feel Like a Woman" By Shania Twain	Mayhem Miller
6	Blair St. Clair vs. The Vixen	"I'm Coming Out" By Diana Ross	The Vixen
7	Monique Heart vs. The Vixen	"Cut to the Feeling" By Carly Rae Jepsen	Monique Heart
8	Asia O'Hara vs. The Vixen	"Groove Is in the Heart" By Deee-Lite	The Vixen
9	Eureka vs. Kameron Michaels	"New Attitude" By Patti LaBelle	No Elimination
10	Kameron Michaels vs. Monét X Change	"Good as Hell" By Lizzo	Monét X Change
11	Kameron Michaels vs. Miz Cracker	"Nasty Girl" By Vanity 6	Miz Cracker
12	Aquaria vs. Asia O'Hara vs. Eureka vs. Kameron Michaels	"Call Me Mother" By RuPaul	No Elimination
14 A	Asia O'Hara vs. Kameron Michaels	"Nasty" By Janet Jackson	Asia O'Hara
14 B	Aquaria vs. Eureka	"If" By Janet Jackson	No Elimination
14 C	Aquaria vs. Eureka vs. Kameron Michaels	"Bang Bang" By Jessie J, Ariana Grande and Nicki Minaj	Eureka & Kameron Michaels

All Stars Season 1

EP	CONTESTANTS	SONG	ELIMINATED
1	Team Shad (Shannel & Chad Michaels) vs. Team Mandora (Mimi Imfurst & Pandora Boxx)	"Opposites Attract" By Paula Abdul	Team Mandora (Mimi Imfurst & Pandora Boxx)
2	Team Latrila (Latrice Royale & Manila Luzon) vs. Team Brown Flowers (Tammie Brown & Nina Flowers)	"There's No Business Like Show Business" By Ethel Merman	Team Brown Flowers (Tammie Brown & Nina Flowers)
3	Team Latrila (Latrice Royale & Manila Luzon) vs. Team Rujubee (Jujubee & Raven)	"Nasty" By Janet Jackson	Team Latrila (Latrice Royale & Manila Luzon)
4	Team Yarlexis (Yara Sofia & Alexis Mateo) vs. Team Rujubee (Jujubee & Raven)	"Don't Cha" By The Pussycat Dolls	Team Yarlexis (Yara Sofia & Alexis Mateo)
5	Jujubee vs. Raven	"Dancing on My Own" By Robyn	No Elimination
6	Chad Michaels vs. Raven	"Responsitrannity (Matt's Pop Edit)" By RuPaul	Raven

All Stars Season 2
Lip Sync for Your Legacy

EP	CONTESTANTS	SONG	ELIMINATED
1	Roxxxy Andrews vs. Tatianna	"Shake It Off" By Taylor Swift	Coco Montrese
2	Alaska vs. Katya	"Le Freak (Freak Out)" By Chic	Tatianna
3	Alyssa Edwards vs. Detox	"Tell It to My Heart" By Taylor Dayne	Ginger Minj
4	Alaska vs. Phi Phi O'Hara	"Got to Be Real" By Cheryl Lynn	Alyssa Edwards
5	Alyssa Edwards vs. Tatianna	"Shut Up & Drive" By Rihanna	Phi Phi O'Hara
6	Alaska vs. Katya	"Cherry Bomb" By Joan Jett & The Blackhearts	Tatianna
7	Detox vs. Katya	"Step It Up" By RuPaul ft. Dave Aude	Alyssa Edwards
8	Alaska vs. Detox vs. Katya	"If I Were Your Woman" By Gladys Knight and the Pips	Detox & Katya

All Stars Season 3
Lip Sync for Your Legacy

EP	CONTESTANTS	SONG	ELIMINATED
1	Aja vs. BenDeLaCreme	"Anaconda" By Nikki Minaj	Morgan McMichaels
2	BenDeLaCreme vs. Shangela	"Jump" By The Pointer Sisters	Thorgy Thor
3	BenDeLaCreme vs. Kennedy Davenport	"Green Light" By Lorde	Milk
4	BenDeLaCreme vs. Shangela	"I Kissed a Girl" By Katy Perry	Chi Chi DeVayne
5	BeBe Zahara Benet vs. Trixie Mattel	"The Boss" By Diana Ross	Aja
6	BeBe Zahara Benet vs. BenDeLaCreme	"Nobody's Supposed to Be Here (Hex Hector Dance Mix)" By Deborah Cox	BenDeLaCreme
7	Shangela vs. Trixie Mattel	"Freaky Money" By RuPaul ft. Big Freedia	Morgan McMichaels
8	Kennedy Davenport vs. Trixie Mattel	"Wrecking Ball" By Miley Cyrus	Kennedy Davenport

All Stars Season 4
Lip Sync for Your Legacy

EP	CONTESTANTS	SONG	ELIMINATED
1	Monique Heart vs. Trinity the Tuck	"Emotions" By Mariah Carey	Jasmine Masters
2	Monét X Change vs. Valentina	"Into You" By Ariana Grande	Farrah Moan
3	Manila Luzon vs. Trinity the Tuck	"How Will I Know?" By Whitney Houston	Gia Gunn
4	Manila Luzon vs. Monique Heart	"The Bitch Is Back" By Tina Turner	Latrice Royale
5	Manila Luzon vs. Monét X Change	"Jump to It" By Aretha Franklin	No Elimination
6A	Jasmine Masters vs. Trinity the Tuck	"Peanut Butter" By RuPaul ft. Big Freedia	Jasmine Masters
6B	Farrah Moan vs. Valentina	"Kitty Girl" By RuPaul	Farrah Moan
6C	Gia Gunn vs. Naomi Smalls	"Adrenaline" By RuPaul	Gia Gunn
6D	Latrice Royale vs. Monique Heart	"Sissy That Walk" By RuPaul	No Elimination Latrice Royale returned
7	Latrice Royale vs. Trinity the Tuck	"You Spin Me Right Round (Like a Record)" By Dead or Alive	Valentina
8	Monét X Change vs. Naomi Smalls	"Come Rain or Come Shine" By Judy Garland	Manila Luzon
9	Monique Heart vs. Trinity the Tuck	"When I Think of You" By Janet Jackson	Latrice Royale
10	Monét X Change vs. Trinity the Tuck	"Fighter" By Christina Aguilera	No Elimination

Published in 2019
by Smith Street Books
Melbourne | Australia
smithstreetbooks.com

ISBN: 978-1-925811-09-4

All rights reserved. No part of this book may be reproduced or transmitted by any person or entity, in any form or means, electronic or mechanical, including photocopying, recording, scanning or by any storage and retrieval system, without the prior written permission of the publishers and copyright holders.

Copyright text © John Davis
Copyright illustrations © Paul Borchers
Copyright design © Smith Street Books

CIP data is available from the NLA.

Publisher: Paul McNally
Editor: Ariana Klepac
Design concept: Murray Batten
Layout: Heather Menzies
Writer: John Davis
Illustrator: Paul Borchers

Printed & bound in China by C&C Offset Printing Co., Ltd.

Book 88
10 9 8 7 6 5 4 3 2 1